THE
LION IN
WINTER

JAMES GOLDMAN

A DELL BOOK

DELL PUBLISHING CO., INC.
750 Third Avenue
New York, New York 10017

Copyright © 1968 by James Goldman

Dell ® TM 681510, Dell Publishing Co., Inc.

Printed in U.S.A.

First printing—October 1968
Second printing—April 1969

THE
LION IN
WINTER

A WORD ABOUT CASTLES

The Lion in Winter was a special and peculiar sort of history play. To make its style and intention clear on film, the look of the castle where it occurs and the sense of castle life need to be earthily realistic and, at the same time, strikingly different from what we're used to seeing in King Arthur movies.

Almost nothing is known about the castle at Chinon as it was in Henry's time; and little enough is known about twelfth-century castles in general. One thing is clear, however, and important for our purposes: namely, that such castles looked nothing like what we expect.

The stone fortresses that remain today were only the shell of castles as they were lived in. Most of the shelter for most of the staff, all of the workshops—the armories, forges, stables and so on—were made of wood. A castle courtyard was a crowded, teeming, dirty place with much more wood than stone to greet the eye.

A major castle, as Chinon was, was like a miniature town. Everything necessary to the life of the establishment existed inside the walls. Poultry, livestock, looms and tailors, mills for grinding grain, vast storerooms, water wells, boot makers, gardens—everything vital to life under siege was somehow packed in.

At special times, like the Christmas Court during which the film occurs, the congestion was even worse than usual. All guests, the visiting nobles and clergymen, traveled with trains of varying size. So, in addition to the usual crowding, we find hundreds of soldiers and servants living outdoors, jammed together in tents, huddling for warmth around dozens of fires.

Living conditions, even for royalty, were crude and rough. The castle rooms were spartan: a bed, a few chairs, chests for storage, clothes hung in the open on racks. Floors were covered with straw, which was swept away and replaced only occasionally. Interiors at high noon on a clear day were always dark, illumination coming from extremely smoky torches and candles. In winter, wind whistled through the open slit windows and the place was freezing cold.

A lot of the habits of the time seem oddly contradictory. In spite of the cold, everyone from the king to his vassal slept naked. In the midst of the general crudeness, nobles wore the most exquisite fabrics—cloths of gold and silver, delicate brocades. Clothing was generally dirty and even at a Christmas Court, nothing looked clean. Tables were set with fine linen, and napkins of a kind were used; yet most of the eating was done with fingers. Sanitary conditions were appalling. For some reason, castles, in addition to their human tenants, were populated by hundreds of dogs.

All these things—the grime and dirt and cold, the coarseness and crudity of life in general—are vital to the look of the film. On the whole, there are few specific references to these elements in the screenplay. Rather than clutter up the goings on with data, it seemed better to suggest them here and let the castle that the story moves in be imagined.

THE CHARACTERS

HENRY II, *King of England; age 50*

ELEANOR OF AQUITAINE, *his wife; age 61*

RICHARD THE LIONHEARTED, *their oldest boy; age 26*

GEOFFREY, *their middle boy; age 25*

JOHN, *their youngest boy; age 16*

ALAIS CAPET, *a French princess; age 23*

PHILIP CAPET, *the King of France; age 18*

WILLIAM MARSHAL, *a noted soldier and friend of the family; age about 35*

THE TIME: *Christmas, 1183*

THE PLACE: *Henry's castle at Chinon, France*

THE LION IN WINTER

(Blue sky. A few light clouds. A bird flies past. We follow it, then suddenly veer down and see HENRY PLANTAGENET close up: His eyes are bright, his teeth bared in a grin of fierce excitement. He is poised for dueling, sword in hand.

(HENRY is 50, an age at which, in his time, men were either old or dead. Not HENRY. Very nearly all he ever was, he is enjoying that final rush of physical and mental vigor that comes to some men not before the end but just before the start of the decline.

(The story starts as HENRY barks out:)

HENRY

Come on. Come for me.

(He brings his sword down and the duel begins. His OPPONENT, whom we see from behind, charges at him, raining blow after blow. HENRY parries only, never striking back, always retreating.

(They fight across the field. Suddenly, HENRY, moving backwards, trips and falls. With a cry, his OPPONENT charges at him. Effortlessly, HENRY strikes his first blow. The OPPONENT's sword flies from his hand as he sprawls flat on the ground. HENRY bounds to his feet, moves to his fallen opponent, looks down, and we see—

(JOHN, his son of 16, who, in 18 years, was to

become the worst king in English history. Still
pudgy with baby fat, he has a round open face that
is enchanting when he smiles. He is frightened now
and shaken up. HENRY glares down, sword in hand.
Then, with a quick, gruff smile, he reaches down
and yanks JOHN to his feet.)

HENRY

You're gaining on it, Johnny.

JOHN

Am I, Father? Am I really?

HENRY

Off you go, now. Run along and practice.

(JOHN picks up his sword, starts across the field
toward a KNIGHT, his dueling master, who stands
waiting. HENRY, a look of affection on his face as
he looks after JOHN, turns and starts across the
field toward the little tent. He waves. We can
just make out a figure by the tent. It waves back.)

(We see JOHN and the KNIGHT. JOHN casts a look
in HENRY's direction. There is no love lost. He
turns back and dueling practice begins.

(In a tent, food for a royal picnic is hand-
somely arranged. The figure we saw is a girl.
HENRY lies, his head on her lap.

(We see the GIRL, close up. ALAIS CAPET is 23 and
exquisitely beautiful. She is like a fine porcelain
figure—fragile, delicate, pure, the only person in
this story easy to break. She is happily and desper-
ately in love with HENRY; it's all over her as she
looks down at him.)

ALAIS

(Singing softly in her native tongue; bright and
gay.)

Allons gai, gai, gai, bergère; allons gai.

Allons gai, soyez legère, suivez moi.

     (HENRY's gaze is out across the field.)

HENRY

He'll make a good king. He'll be ready.

     (For a moment we see JOHN and the KNIGHT:
     JOHN flailing away, stumbles and staggers about.)
That's it, that's the way, lad.

ALAIS

Have you found religion, Henry? Will you look down from the clouds and see who's sitting on your throne?

HENRY

     (He sits up, takes a chicken leg from a platter,
     starts devouring it.)
I've got to know before I die. There is a legend of a king called Lear, with whom I have a lot in common. Both of us have kingdoms and three children we adore and both of us are old. But there it stops. He cut his kingdom into bits. I can't do that. I've built an empire: all of England, half of France. I am the greatest power in a thousand years and after me comes John.

ALAIS

I'm going to lose you, Henry, aren't I?

HENRY

Alais, in my time, I've known contessas, milkmaids, courtesans and novices, whores, gypsies, jades and little boys, but nowhere in God's western world have I found anyone to love but you.

ALAIS

And Rosamund.

HENRY

She's dead.

ALAIS

And Eleanor.

HENRY

The new Medusa, my good wife.

ALAIS

How is your queen?

HENRY

Decaying, I suppose. No, don't be jealous of the gorgon; she
is not among the things I love. How many husbands do you
know who lock their wives away? I haven't kept the great
bitch in the keep for ten years out of passionate attachment.

(He sees something across the field.)

Ah, there's Captain Marshal.

(He rises, beckons, calls.)

William.

(Across the field, on horseback, riding past them
toward Henry, is WILLIAM MARSHAL.

(He is 35 and looks like the distinguished soldier
he is. A rugged face but honest, open and friendly.
He was totally devoted to Henry and his children
and through all their wars and conflicts somehow
managed always to be loyal to all of them.

(HENRY smiles as MARSHAL stands before him,
bowing.)

HENRY

We will be holding Christmas Court at Chinon. We have
asked the King of France to join us. I want Richard there.
And Geoffrey. Find my boys and tell them so. And then go
fetch the Queen from Salisbury Tower.

MARSHAL

If the Queen refuses?

HENRY

Eleanor? She wouldn't miss this for the world.

(MARSHAL nods, moves toward his horse. The
horse whinnies.)

I'm afraid it's going to be a family Christmas.

death below but at a maneuver nicely done.

(MARSHAL appears behind him. He speaks quietly.)

MARSHAL

Geoffrey.

GEOFFREY

(Turning to MARSHAL.)

Father wants to see me.

(MARSHAL nods.)

Where and when?

(Dark, rolling late autumnal countryside. A castle on a hilltop in the distance. MARSHAL rides past us toward the castle.)

(Then we're in a large, cold, relatively barren castle room. A few chairs, wooden chests, a bed, a few wall tapestries, straw on the floor. The camera takes in the room. Two MAIDS-IN-WAITING sit huddled by the fire, doing needlework. Perched on a high stool by the room's one slit of a window sits ELEANOR OF AQUITAINE. She is 61 and looks nothing like it. She is a truly handsome woman of great temperament, authority and presence. She has been a queen of international importance for 46 years and you know it. Finally, she is that most unusual thing: a genuinely feminine woman thoroughly capable of holding her own in a man's world.

(She has been painting an exquisite miniature on ivory. She still holds the brush but is motionless now, listening to the unbolting of the door. Her face shows nothing.)

MARSHAL

Your majesty.

ELEANOR

There is to be a Christmas Court.

MARSHAL

(Voice over.)

Yes, madam.

ELEANOR

Where?

> (Nothing but her face. The look is enigmatic
> but the excitement is unmistakable)

MARSHAL

At Chinon.

> (We see the castle in the dim gray light of pre-
> dawn. It is winter now. Mist rises. In the castle
> yard, no signs of life. Silence. A dog walks by.
>
> (Then, veering up, we see the rising sun. Its first
> rays strike the top of the bell tower. The bell starts
> to swing. Its clapper comes crashing down.
>
> (A large bowl of water. Ice has formed across the
> top. Two hands come smashing through the ice.
>
> (We're in HENRY's bedroom. Bare, spartan, cold;
> no elegance at all. HENRY, half-dressed, stands be-
> fore the bowl of water. ALAIS, blankets clutched
> around her, sits on the bed. She speaks.)

ALAIS

Henry, what if, just for once, I didn't do as I was told?

HENRY

(Splashing water on his face:)

It's going to be a jungle of a day. If I start growling now,
I'll never last.

> (ALAIS, on the bed, robe over her shoulders, is
> starting to dress.)

ALAIS

You'll last. You're like the rocks at Stonehenge. Nothing
knocks you down.

HENRY

(Drying his face with a towel.)

In these rooms, Alais, on this Christmas, I have all the enemies I need.

ALAIS

You have more than you think.

HENRY

Are you one? Has my willow turned to poison oak?

ALAIS

If I decided to be trouble, Henry, how much trouble could I be?

HENRY

Not much.

> (HENRY and ALAIS, dressed now, are moving down a corridor. They pass an occasional SERVANT, who stops and bows. We follow them as HENRY strides briskly along, ALAIS half-running to keep up.)

ALAIS

I could give away your plans.

HENRY

You don't know what they are.

ALAIS

I know you want to disinherit Richard.

HENRY

So does Eleanor. She knows young Henry's dead. The Young King died in summer and I haven't named an heir. She knows I want John on the throne and I know she wants Richard. We are very frank about it.

> (HENRY and ALAIS are at a table eating breakfast. They eat, as was the custom, with spoons and fingers from a common bowl that sits on the table between them.)

ALAIS

Henry, I can't be your mistress if I'm married to your son.

HENRY

Why can't you? Johnny wouldn't mind.

ALAIS

I do not like your Johnny.

HENRY

He's a good boy.

ALAIS

He's got pimples and he smells of compost.

HENRY

He's just sixteen; he can't help the pimples.

ALAIS

He could have a bath.

> (HENRY is striding briskly down a corridor,
> ALAIS hurrying after him. The corridor is more
> crowded now. There are KNIGHTS and HIGH CLERGY-
> MEN who, as HENRY passes, stop and bow. HENRY
> ignores it all, striding on until he reaches a niche
> in the corridor. He stops abruptly, turns on ALAIS.)

HENRY

It isn't such a dreadful thing to be a queen of England.
Not all eyes will weep for you.

ALAIS

Will yours?

HENRY

I don't know. Very likely.

ALAIS

All I want is not to lose you. Can't you hide me? Can't I
simply disappear?

HENRY

You know you can't. Your little brother Philip's King of
France now and he wants your wedding or your dowry
back. I only took you for your dowry. You were seven; two
big knees and two big eyes and that's all. How was I to
know?

(We pull back as HENRY moves to kiss her lightly.
There is a sound of running down the corridor. It's
JOHN. He slows down as he sees his father and
fiancée kissing. He doesn't like it. Sensing someone, HENRY turns, takes JOHN in.)

What's wrong, lad?

                        JOHN
        (Producing a smile.)

Nothing.

        (With a skip and a wave, JOHN resumes running
down the corridor. We follow him as he turns a
corner, reaches a great high door, tugs it open, slips
through and starts racing down a broad exterior
flight of steps into the castle yard. Calling, waving,
excited and happy:)

Geoff! Geoff!

        (We see the yard. GEOFFREY, on horseback, is rid-
ing toward us. He waves back. The yard is a mob
scene, crammed with SOLDIERS, SERVANTS, PEASANTS,
tents, outdoor kitchens, livestock, poultry, horses,
the lot. The SOLDIERS are lined up for morning
chow.

        (JOHN threads his way through it all, reaching
GEOFFREY as he dismounts)

                        GEOFFREY
        (As they hug each other roughly.)

Johnny.

                        JOHN
        (A large bundle hangs from GEOFFREY's saddle.
Pointing to it.)

Is that for me?

                (GEOFFREY nods.)

I love Christmas.

(An enormous Christmas tree, close up, is being raised to standing position.

(HENRY nods at the tree in brisk approval. ALAIS stands near him, wanting to speak but hesitant. We are in the parlor, a fairly spacious place which functioned as a kind of family room. There are the usual tapestries, some furniture, a desk and, scattered about, piles of holly boughs.

(HENRY turns to leave the room. ALAIS stops him, saying:)

ALAIS

What difference does my dowry make? Let Philip have it back. It isn't much.

HENRY

I can't. The Vexin is a little county but it's vital to me.

ALAIS

And I'm not.

HENRY

It's been my luck to fall in love with landed women. When I married Eleanor, I thought: "You lucky man. The richest woman in the world. She owns the Aquitaine, the greatest province on the Continent—and beautiful as well." She was, you know.

ALAIS

And you adored her.

HENRY

Memory fails. There may have been an era when I did.
(He arranges a loose lock of her hair.)
Let's have one strand askew; nothing in life has any business being perfect. If I say you and I are done, we're done. If I say marry John, it's John. I'll have you by me and I'll use you as I like.

(JOHN and GEOFFREY, in the courtyard, turn at

a great clatter of horse's hooves behind them. They stop and turn.

(RICHARD arrives in the yard at full gallop. He reins in with great bravado and leaps from his horse.

(GEOFFREY starts toward RICHARD with a friendly wave of greeting. JOHN, glaring sullenly at RICHARD, hangs back, then follows GEOFFREY.

(We see RICHARD, JOHN and GEOFFREY crossing the courtyard toward the stables. RICHARD leads his horse.)

GEOFFREY

Ah, Christmas; warm and rosy time. The hot wine steams, the Yule log roars and we're the fat that's in the fire. She'll be here soon, you know.

JOHN

Who?

RICHARD

Mother.

GEOFFREY

Does she still want you to be king?

RICHARD

We are not as friendly as we were.

JOHN

If I'm supposed to make a fuss and kiss her hairy cheek, I won't.

RICHARD

What you kiss, little prince, is up to you.

JOHN

I'm Father's favorite; that's what counts.

RICHARD

(Stopping, looking down at JOHN, with quiet, total conviction.)

You hardly know me, Johnny, so I beg you to believe my reputation. I'm a constant soldier and a sometime poet and I will be king.

JOHN

Just you remember: Father loves me best.

(HENRY is seated at a desk, busily going through state papers. ALAIS hovers about.)

ALAIS

Why John? John doesn't care for you at all.

HENRY

We love each other deeply.

ALAIS

None of them has any love for you.

HENRY

Because we fight? Tell me they all three want the crown, I'll tell you it's a feeble prince that doesn't. They may snap at me and plot and that makes them the kind of sons I want. I've snapped and plotted all my life. There is no other way to be a king, alive and fifty all at once.

ALAIS

I'm going to fight for you.

HENRY

Oh, fine.

(We're on the walk that runs along the top of the castle wall. HENRY is pacing impatiently, repeatedly looking out in expectation toward the River Vienne, which runs quite near, below them. Suddenly, excitedly, he points.)

Look.

(A boat rounds a bend in the river near the castle.
(ELEANOR is enthroned on the deck of the boat.
MARSHAL stands near her. ELEANOR'S GUARD, on duty,

stands stiffly in the background. ELEANOR'S TWO
MAIDS-IN-WAITING stand near him.

(HENRY hurries down stone castle steps. His face
is lit with a sense of eagerness and anticipation that
have nothing to do with affection.

(The boat is near the dock now. ELEANOR'S face
is alive with suppressed excitement. She pats her
hair, finds it in order, anxiously tugs at her cloak.

(HENRY strides through the turmoil of the castle
yard. Far behind him, ALAIS hurries after.

(We move back and forth between HENRY and
ELEANOR. She edges forward, eager, on her throne.
He stomps through the bracken and the muck
along the river bank. Sailors throw ropes. The boat
glides firmly home through the mud. The Oarsmen raise their oars in salute as, rising, she strides
down the boat to land and HENRY.)

HENRY

How was your crossing? Did the Channel part for you?

ELEANOR

It went flat when I told it to. I didn't think to ask for more.
How dear of you to let me out of jail.

HENRY

It's only for the holidays.

ELEANOR

Like school. You keep me young.

(They turn, start up the dock toward the castle.
She sees ALAIS.)

Here's gentle Alais.

(ALAIS starts to curtsy.)

No, no; greet me as you used to.

(She takes ALAIS into her arms, holding her
lightly.)

Fragile I am not; affection is a pressure I can bear.

> (As she releases ALAIS, she looks up toward the
> castle. JOHN, RICHARD and GEOFFREY are standing
> there, by the main gate.)

Oh, but I do have handsome children.

> (She busses JOHN on the cheek. We pull back
> and see that they are in the parlor.)

John—you're so clean and neat. Henry takes good care of
you.

> (She moves to RICHARD, kisses him lightly.)

And Richard. Don't look sullen, dear. It makes your eyes go
small and piggy and your chin look weak. Is Philip here?

GEOFFREY

Not yet.

ELEANOR

Let's hope he's grown up like his father—simon pure and
simon simple. Good, good Louis; if I'd managed sons for
him instead of all those little girls, I'd still be stuck with
being Queen of France and we should not have known each
other. Such, my angels, is the role of sex in history.

> (Great flourishes on horns and trumpets are
> heard from the castle yard.)

That will be Philip.

> (She turns and starts toward the door.
>
> (We pick her up crossing a hallway by some
> stairs, her boys strung out behind her. She slows,
> pauses, looks around expectantly.)

Where's Henry?

RICHARD

Upstairs with the family whore.

ELEANOR

That is a mean and tawdry way to talk about your fiancée.

JOHN

My fiancée.

ELEANOR

Whoever fiancée, I brought her up and she is dear to me and gentle.

RICHARD

He still plans to make John king.

ELEANOR

Of course he does. My, what a greedy little trinity you are: king, king, king. Two of you must learn to live with disappointment.

(HENRY strides toward them.)

HENRY

Ah, but which two?

ELEANOR

Let's deny them all and live forever.

HENRY

Tusk to tusk through all eternity.

(TWO SERVANTS approach bearing a crown and a great formal cloak. Briskly, to his boys, as he shrugs into the cloak and claps the crown on:)

The King of France and I will shortly have a tactile conversation, like two surgeons looking for a lump. We'll state positions and I'll make the first of many offers. He'll refuse it, naturally, I'll make a better one and so on through the holidays until I win. For the duration of this joyous ritual, you will give, to your father, your support.

(With which he wheels toward the door. The TWO SERVANTS throw it open and HENRY, the others following, strides forward into the courtyard.

(We see a very grand and formal state occasion. NOBLES and CLERGYMEN stand in formal ranks along the broad descending steps. All the COMMON FOLK have lined up, as common folk always do, along the edges of a broad aisle. SOLDIERS, at attention, line the aisle.

(Down the aisle marches a gorgeous, stately retinue of KNIGHTS and SOLDIERS. At their head is Philip, King of France. PHILIP CAPET is 18 years old and absolutely gorgeous. He is tall, well proportioned and handsome without being at all pretty. His manner is open, direct, simple and strikingly authoritative. He has been King of France for three years and has learned a lot.)

HENRY

(As they greet each other.)

My lord.

PHILIP

Your grace.

HENRY

Welcome to Chinon.

(More horns and trumpets as HENRY turns.

(The door of the parlor, seen from inside the room. The door flies open and HENRY bursts in, ELEANOR and PHILIP just behind him. There is a general change of manner, from formal to informal, as RICHARD, GEOFFREY, JOHN and ALAIS follow into the room.

(HENRY takes off his formal robe, feeling more comfortable.)

Well, that's better.

ELEANOR

(To PHILIP.)

I was told you were impressive for a boy of seventeen. I'm Eleanor, who might have been your mother. All the others here you know.

PHILIP

(Bowing.)

Queen Eleanor.

HENRY

(Informal, settling himself comfortably in a chair.)

I gather you're disturbed about your sister and her dowry.

PHILIP

(Standing before him, stiff and formal.)

Sixteen years ago, you made a treaty with us. It is time its terms were executed.

(The scene, through most of the following exchange between Philip and Henry, is a domestic one. ALAIS passes among them with a tray of drinks and hors d'oeuvres. ELEANOR settles comfortably, takes some needlework from a bag and works at it. JOHN busies himself decking the hall with boughs of holly. GEOFFREY, finding the hors d'oeuvres delicious, settles by a table that holds an assortment of them. Only RICHARD fails to relax. He stands apart from all of them, suspicious and hostile.)

HENRY

I should think so.

PHILIP

Our position comes to this: that you either hold the marriage or return the Vexin. Alais marries Richard or we'll have the county back at once.

HENRY

That's clear, concise and well presented. My position is— well, frankly, Philip, it's a tangle.

(As he rises and moves to RICHARD, all affability.)

Two years ago, the Queen and I, for reasons passing understanding, gave the Aquitaine to Richard. That makes Richard very powerful. How can I give him Alais, too? The man she marries has you for an ally.

PHILIP

It's their wedding or the Vexin back. Those are the terms you made with Louis.

HENRY

(Moving to PHILIP. Just the two of them now.)
True but academic, lad. The Vexin's mine.

PHILIP

By what authority?

HENRY

It's got my troops all over it: that makes it mine. Now hear me, boy—

PHILIP

I am a king: I'm no man's boy.

HENRY

A king? Because you put your ass on purple cushions?

PHILIP

Sir.

(He turns on his heel, starts for the door.
(HENRY and ELEANOR exchange amused glances.)

HENRY

Philip, you haven't got the feel of this at all. Use all your voices. When I bellow, bellow back.

PHILIP

I'll mark that down.

HENRY

(Moving close to PHILIP.)
This, too. We are the world in small. A nation is a human thing. It does what we do, for our reasons. Surely, if we're civilized, it must be possible to put the knives away. We can make peace. We have it in our hands.

PHILIP

I've tutors of my own. Will that be all?

HENRY

Oh, think. You came here for a reason. Don't you want to ask me if I've got an offer?

PHILIP

Have you got an offer?

HENRY

Not yet—but I'll think of one.

(PHILIP is half out the door.)

Oh, by the way . . .

(PHILIP turns. HENRY smiles agreeably.)

You're better at this than I thought you'd be.

(PHILIP smiles agreeably back.)

PHILIP

I wasn't sure you'd noticed.

(PHILIP goes. HENRY turns, taking in his family.

(We see JOHN with holly, ELEANOR with her needle, GEOFFREY licking his fingers, ALAIS serving more wine and RICHARD glowering.

(HENRY makes a friendly, expansive gesture.)

HENRY

Well—what shall we hang? The holly or each other?

RICHARD

(Moving into the picture.)

Would you say, Father, that I have the makings of a king?

HENRY

A splendid king.

RICHARD

Would you expect me, Father, to give up without a fight?

HENRY

Of course you'll fight. I raised you to.

RICHARD

I don't care what you offer Philip. I don't care what plans you make. I'll have the Aquitaine and Alais and the crown.

I won't give up one to get the other. I won't trade off Alais or the Aquitaine to this—

>(He gestures toward JOHN.)

—this walking pustule.

>(We see JOHN's outrage.)

No, your loving son will not.

>(As he turns to go, JOHN rushes up to HENRY.)

JOHN

Did you hear what he called me?

ELEANOR

Clearly, dear. Now run along. It's nearly dinnertime.

JOHN

I only do what Father tells me.

HENRY

Go and eat.

JOHN

Did I say something wrong? I'm always saying something wrong.

HENRY

Don't pout.

JOHN

>(Pouting.)

I'm not.

HENRY

>(Giving him a slap on the butt.)

And stand up straight. How often do I have to tell you?

>(JOHN scurries toward the door.
>(HENRY, the exasperated parent, sighs.
>(ELEANOR gazes with amusement at HENRY.)

ELEANOR

And that's to be the king.

GEOFFREY

And I'm to be his chancellor. Has he told you? John will

rule the country while I run it. That's to say, he gets to
spend the taxes that I get to raise.

ELEANOR

How nice for you.

GEOFFREY

It's not as nice as being king.

HENRY

We've made you Duke of Brittany. Is that so little?

GEOFFREY

No one ever thinks of crowns and mentions Geoff. Why is
that?

HENRY

Isn't being chancellor power enough?

GEOFFREY

It isn't power that I feel deprived of; it's the mention that
I miss. There's no affection for me here. You wouldn't think
I'd want that, would you?

> (He is going as he says this. ELEANOR bleakly
> watches him go.)

ELEANOR

Henry, I have a confession.

HENRY

Yes?

ELEANOR

I don't much like our children.

> (Rising, moving toward ALAIS.)

Only you. The child I raised but didn't bear.

ALAIS

You never cared for me.

ELEANOR

I did and do. Believe me, Henry's bed is Henry's province.
He can people it with sheep for all I care. Which, on occasion, he has done.

(The subject of Rosamund is clearly a raw nerve.)

HENRY

Still that? When Rosamund's been dead for seven years.

ELEANOR

Two months and eighteen days. I never liked her much.

HENRY

You count the days?

ELEANOR

I made the numbers up. He found Miss Clifford in the mists of Wales and brought her home for closer observation. Liking what he saw, he scrutinized her many years. He loved her deeply and she him. And yet, my dear, when Henry had to choose between his lady and my lands . . .

ALAIS

There is no sport in hurting me. It is so easy.

ELEANOR

After all the years of love and care, do you think I could bring myself to hurt you?

ALAIS

Eleanor, with both hands tied behind you.

(We see HENRY, as ALAIS turns and goes. His concern for her is clearly on his face.)

HENRY

She is lovely, isn't she.

ELEANOR

Yes: very.

HENRY

(Joining her.)

If I'd chosen, who could I have picked to love to gall you more?

ELEANOR

(Smiling up at him.)

There's no one.

(She settles by the Christmas tree. HENRY joins
her. He fiddles with a Christmas ornament, then
hangs it as they talk.)

HENRY

Time hasn't done a thing but wrinkle you.

ELEANOR

It hasn't even done that. I have borne six girls, five boys and
thirty-one connubial years of you. How am I possible?

HENRY

There are moments when I miss you.

ELEANOR

Many?

HENRY

Do you doubt it?

ELEANOR

(Reaching out and tousling his hair.)

That's my wooly sheep dog. So wee Johnny gets the crown.

HENRY

I've heard it rumored but I don't believe it.

ELEANOR

Losing Alais will be hard, for you do love her.

HENRY

It's an old man's last attachment; nothing more. How hard
do you find living in your castle?

ELEANOR

It was difficult in the beginning but that's past. I find I've
seen the world enough.

HENRY

I'll never let you loose. You led too many civil wars against
me.

ELEANOR

And I damn near won the last one. Still, as long as I get
trotted out for Christmas Courts and state occasions now

and then, for I do like to see you, it's enough. I'm famished.
Let's go in to dinner.

HENRY

(Extending his arm.)
Arm in arm.

ELEANOR

And hand in hand.
                    (She takes his arm. They start out of the room.)
You're still a marvel of a man.

HENRY

And you're my lady.
                    (He opens the door, moves into the corridor. She
                    follows. We go with them down the hallway. It is
                    dimly lit by smoky wall torches. The corridor is
                    empty except for occasional, quietly prowling dogs.)
It's an odd thing, Eleanor. I've fought and bargained all
these years as if the only thing I lived for was what happened after I was dead. I've something else to live for now.
I've blundered on to peace.

ELEANOR

(Wry amusement on her face.)
On Christmas Eve.

HENRY

Since Louis died, while Philip grew, I've had no France to
fight. And in that lull, I've found how good it is to write a
law or make a tax more fair or sit in judgment to decide
which peasant gets a cow. There is, I tell you, nothing more
important in the world. And now the French boy's big
enough and I am sick of war.

ELEANOR

Do you still need the Vexin, Henry?

HENRY

It's as crucial as it ever was. My troops there are a day away
from Paris, just a march of twenty miles. I must keep it.

ELEANOR

Henry, dear, if Alais doesn't marry Richard, I will see you lose the Vexin.

> (They stop outside a large double door.)

HENRY

Well, I thought you'd never say it.

ELEANOR

I can do it.

HENRY

You can try.

> (A SERVANT appears, moves to the door.)

We've got a pack of barons we should look the loving couple for.

ELEANOR

> (Smiling a terrible smile at him.)

Can you read love in that?

HENRY

And permanent affection.

> (The door is opened. They start forward into—
> (The castle's Great Hall. It is an enormous, high-ceilinged, stone-walled room. Long trestle tables run the length of it. NOBLES and CLERGYMEN sit on benches at the tables. COURT MUSICIANS and ENTERTAINERS are poised on a platform at one side. SERVANTS stand formally at serving tables piled high with food. The royal table is at the far end of the hall on a platform. PHILIP, RICHARD, GEOFFREY, JOHN and ALAIS are there.
> (The hall is heated by a huge fire that blazes on the stone floor in the center of the room. Some of the smoke rises to escape from a hole in the ceiling. Torches are everywhere. The smoke is terrible. There is much howling from a multitude of dogs.

(As HENRY and ELEANOR move into the hall, the orchestra plays a fanfare and everybody rises.

ELEANOR

(As she and HENRY make their stately way down the long hall to their table, nodding to this noble, smiling at that one.)

My Richard is the next king, not your John. I know you, Henry. I know every twist and bend you've got and I'll be waiting round each corner for you.

HENRY

Do you truly care who's king?

ELEANOR

I care because you care so much.

HENRY

Don't fight me, Eleanor.

ELEANOR

What would you have me do? Give out, give up, give in?

HENRY

Give me a little peace.

ELEANOR

A little? Why so modest? How about eternal peace? Now there's a thought.

HENRY

If you oppose me, I will strike you any way I can.

(They have reached their table. Their eyes are locked; HENRY's cold with warning, ELEANOR's bright with defiance.

(The pose breaks and they sit. SERVANTS appear by each of them with bowls of water and towels. They start to wash their hands. Then:)

ELEANOR

(She leans toward HENRY. They are close enough to kiss.)

Henry?

HENRY

Madam?

ELEANOR

Did you ever love me?

HENRY

No.

ELEANOR

Good. That will make this pleasanter.

> (She sits back, wipes her hands. We draw away
> from her, taking in more and more of the hall until
> we see all of it—the bustle and smoke, the howling
> and shouting, the music and caroling.

> (We see a Christmas present, wrapped up, tied
> and tagged. ELEANOR is carrying it to a table piled
> with presents in a corner of her bedroom. As she
> puts it down, a door behind her opens and RICH-
> ARD appears. Aware he's there, she studiously in-
> spects the writing on a tag. He waits, then moves
> toward her saying:)

RICHARD

All right. I've come. I'm here. What was it you wanted?

ELEANOR

Just to talk. We haven't been alone, the two of us in—how
long is it, lamb? Two years? You look fit. War agrees with
you. I keep informed. I follow all your slaughters from a
distance. Do sit down.

RICHARD

Is this an audience, a good-night hug with kisses or an am-
bush?

ELEANOR

Let us hope it's a reunion. Must you look so stern? I sent
for you to say I want your love again, but I can't say it to a
face like that.

RICHARD

My love, of all things. What would you want it for?

ELEANOR

Why, for itself. What other purpose could I have?

RICHARD

You'll tell me when you're ready to.

ELEANOR

I scheme a lot; I know. I plot and plan. That's how a queen
in prison spends her time. But there is more to me than that.
Can't I say I love a son and be believed?

RICHARD

If I were you, I'd try another tack. I have no dammed-up
flood of passion for you. There's no chance I'll overflow.

ELEANOR

You are a dull boy. Dull as plainsong: la, la, la, forever on
one note. I gave the Church up out of boredom. I can do as
much for you.

RICHARD

You'll never give me up—not while I hold the Aquitaine.

ELEANOR

You think I'm motivated by a love of real estate.

RICHARD

I think you want it back. You're so deceitful you can't ask
for water when you're thirsty. We could tangle spiders in the
webs you weave.

ELEANOR

If I'm so devious, why don't you go? Don't stand there
quivering in limbo. Love me, little lamb, or leave me.

RICHARD

(Not moving.)
Leave you, Madam? With pure joy.

ELEANOR

Departure is a simple act. You put the left foot down and
then the right.

(JOHN runs into the room, excited in high spirits. GEOFFREY follows him.)

JOHN

Mother—

ELEANOR

Hush, dear. Mother's fighting.

JOHN

Father's finished working out the treaty terms.

ELEANOR

(Getting to her feet.)

How nice. Where is your father?

(He is outside in a corner of the courtyard, busy distributing Christmas largesse to the deserving poor. ALAIS is with him. A SERVANT follows them along, pulling a cart filled with roast geese, pastries and such.

(They are in front of a row of wooden hovels that line the high stone castle wall. Gardeners, poultry keepers, smiths and armorers live in these huts. We see them receiving gifts with bows and smiles.

(It is late afternoon and cold. The shadows are sharp and clear. Activity in the yard, when we see it, is slight. SOLDIERS and PEASANTS are settling down by tiny fires, eating and drinking. From across the yard comes the sound of carolers.

ELEANOR

(Voice over.)

There you are.

(HENRY and ALAIS turn.

(ELEANOR, wearing a heavy robe, is crossing the yard toward them. RICHARD, JOHN and GEOFFREY come along behind her.)

Well—have you put the terms to Philip?

HENRY

Not yet, but we're shortly granting him an audience. I hope you'll all attend.

ELEANOR

Are we to know the terms or would you rather tease us?

HENRY

> (He stops handing out food, moves away from the huts and people toward an area where livestock are kept.)

Not at all. The terms are these:

RICHARD

What are you giving up to Philip? What of mine?

JOHN

Whatever you've got goes to me.

GEOFFREY

And what's the nothing Geoffrey gets?

HENRY

For God's sake, boys, you can't all three be king.

RICHARD

All three of us can try.

HENRY

That's pointless now. I want you to succeed me, Richard. Alais and the crown: I give you both.

RICHARD

I've got no sense of humor. If I did, I'd laugh.

HENRY

I mean to do it.

JOHN

What about me? I'm your favorite, I'm the one you love.

HENRY

John, I can't help myself.

> (He takes JOHN, moves him next to RICHARD. JOHN scowls up, RICHARD glowers down)

HENRY

Could you keep anything I gave you? Could you beat him on the field?

JOHN

(Scurrying to his father.)

You could.

HENRY

But John, I won't be there. I'm losing, too. All of my dreams for you are lost.

JOHN

You've led me on.

HENRY

I never meant to.

JOHN

(The tears start to come.)

You're a failure as a father, you know that?

HENRY

I'm sorry, John.

JOHN

(He sinks down to the frozen ground, a sorry little heap. Pigs peer at him curiously from the enclosure just behind him.)

Not yet you're not. But I'll do something terrible and you'll be sorry then.

ELEANOR

Did you rehearse all this or are you improvising?

HENRY

Good God, woman, face the facts.

ELEANOR

Which ones? We've got so many.

HENRY

Power is the only fact. How can I keep him from the crown? He'd only take it if I didn't give it to him.

RICHARD

No—you'd make me fight to get it. I know you; you'd
never give me anything.

HENRY

True; and I haven't. You get Alais and you get the kingdom
but I get the one thing I want most. If you're king, England
stays intact. I get that. It's all yours now—the girl, the
crown, the whole black bloody business. Isn't that enough?

> (HENRY turns and storms away across the court-
> yard. The caroling resumes.

> (The little group stands by the pigsty, watching
> HENRY go. No one moves until—)

ALAIS

I don't know who's to be congratulated. Not me, cetrainly.

> (She looks at them, eyes bright with anger.)

Kings, Queen, knights everywhere you look and I'm the only
pawn. I haven't got a thing to lose. That makes me dan-
gerous.

> (At the brink of tears, she turns and runs away
> from them—not after HENRY, but in another direc-
> tion.)

ELEANOR

Poor child.

JOHN

> (Suffering at the pigsty.)

Poor John—who says "Poor John"? Don't everybody sob at
once. My God, if I went up in flames, there's not a living
soul who'd pee on me to put the fire out.

RICHARD

Let's strike a flint and see.

JOHN

> (Softly, from the heart, the absolute truth.)

You're everything a little brother dreams of, you know that?
I used to dream about you all the time.

ELEANOR

(Arms open.)

Oh, Johnny . . .

JOHN

(Fighting back the tears.)

I'll show you, Eleanor, I haven't lost yet.

(He starts to move off with dignity but can't keep it up. Bursting into tears, he breaks into a run.

(ELEANOR, RICHARD and GEOFFREY start moving thoughtfully across the yard, past squatting figures, small groups of SOLDIERS drinking. Dogs bark. The wind blows.)

GEOFFREY

Well, Mummy, if you want me, here I am.

ELEANOR

John's lost a chancellor, has he?

GEOFFREY

And you've gained one.

ELEANOR

It is a bitter thing your mummy has to say.

GEOFFREY

She doesn't trust me.

(They stop by a stone well in the yard. GEOFFREY perches on it. RICHARD, always wary, stands apart. In the distance, CAROLERS appear, singing something jolly.)

ELEANOR

You must know Henry isn't through with John. He'll keep the Vexin 'til the moon goes blue from cold, and as for Richard's wedding day, we'll see the Second Coming first; the needlework alone can last for years.

GEOFFREY

I know. You know I know, I know you know I know, we know that Henry knows and Henry knows we know it.

We're a knowledgeable family. Will Richard take me for his chancellor or won't he?

ELEANOR

Why are you dropping John?

GEOFFREY

Because you're going to win.

ELEANOR

I haven't yet.

GEOFFREY

You will, with me to help you. I can handle John. He'll swallow anything I tell him and I'll take him by the hand and walk him into the trap you set.

ELEANOR

You're good, you're first class, Geoff. You'd sell John out to me or me to John or—you can tell me—have you found some way of selling everyone to everybody?

GEOFFREY

Not yet, Mummy, but I'm working on it. I don't care who's king, but you and Henry do. I want to watch the two of you go picknicking on one another.

ELEANOR

You've a gift for hating.

GEOFFREY

You're the expert; you should know.

ELEANOR

Dear Lord, you've loved me all these years.

GEOFFREY

Well, God forgive me, I've upset the Queen. Madam, may you rot.

ELEANOR

We need you. Help us.

GEOFFREY

What? And miss the fun of selling you?

—only me. And then Young Henry came and you and all
the other blossoms in my garden.

> (Looking straight at him. We see them both.)

Yes, if I'd been sterile, darling, I'd be happier today.

RICHARD

Is that designed to hurt me?

ELEANOR

What a waste. I've fought with Henry over who comes next,
whose dawn it is and which son gets the sunset and we'll
never live to see it. Look at you. I loved you more than
Henry and it's cost me everything.

RICHARD

What do you want?

ELEANOR

I want us back the way we were.

RICHARD

That's not it.

ELEANOR

All right, then. I want the Aquitaine.

RICHARD

Now that's the mother I remember.

ELEANOR

We can win. I can get you Alais. I can make the marriage
happen—but I've got to have the Aquitaine to do it. I must
have it back.

RICHARD

It's mine. I'll never give it up.

ELEANOR

I'll write my will. "To Richard, everything." Would you believe me then?

> (She starts to go.)

Where's paper?

RICHARD

Paper burns.

(He turns to go.)

ELEANOR

I love you.

RICHARD

You love nothing. You are incomplete. The human parts of you are missing. You're as dead as you are deadly.

ELEANOR

Don't leave me.

RICHARD

You were lovely once. I've seen the pictures.

ELEANOR

Oh, don't you remember how you loved me?

RICHARD

Vaguely.

ELEANOR

We were always hand in hand.

(She thrusts her hand in his.)

That's how it felt.

RICHARD

As coarse and hot as that.

(She snatches her hand away and bares her forearm.)

ELEANOR

This won't burn. I'll scratch a will on this. "To Richard, everything."

(Suddenly there is a long pin in her hand. She draws it savagely across her forearm. It tears the flesh. We see the blood.)

RICHARD

Mother.

(Her arms are open. He comes into them.)

ELEANOR

Remember how I taught you numbers and the lute and poetry?

RICHARD

(Softly, as they hold each other.)

Mother.

ELEANOR

See? You do remember.

> (We draw back from them. We see the garden
> and the hills beyond. The sun touches the scer˙
> with the last warmth of the day and dips beh ˌd
> the hills. We hear a wisp of caroling. The picture
> holds.)

I taught you dancing, too, and languages and all the music
that I knew and how to love what's beautiful. The sun was
warmer then and we were every day together.

> (All at once, sharp, loud and bright, on HENRY
> in close up. He is roaring with laughter. We hear
> other voices laughing.
>
> (We are in the Great Hall. The dining tables
> have been removed and the benches rearranged.
> Seated on them are the NOBLES and CLERICS. They
> are watching a crude pantomime.
>
> (Gesturing toward WILLIAM MARSHAL, who stands
> a few paces behind him, HENRY says—)

HENRY

William.

> (MARSHAL moves to him.)

Tell the French King I'll receive him in the parlor.

MARSHAL

Yes, my lord.

HENRY

In half an hour.

> (We see PHILIP. He is seated at a table, playing
> chess.)

PHILIP

Half an hour. Good.

(We pull back to see GEOFFREY seated at the table
with him. They are in a small, quiet chamber by
an open fire. MARSHAL bows and goes.)

GEOFFREY

(He makes a move, then says in the most con-
versational way:)

Of course, you know there's not a word of truth to Henry's
terms.

PHILIP

If that's a warning, thank you.

GEOFFREY

What if it's an offer?

PHILIP

"What if" is a game for scholars: What if angels sat on
pinheads?

GEOFFREY

What if I were king?

PHILIP

It's your game, Geoff. You play it.

(As GEOFFREY leans forward to speak—

(A grotesque wood-carving fills the screen: an
executioner, axe raised, a victim, head on the block.
The axe, drops. The severed head falls. Drawing
back, we see JOHN, looking with proud approval at
the toy.

(He looks up sharply as GEOFFREY enters.)

GEOFFREY

John—

JOHN

(Attention returning to his model.)

I made this for Father. All the pieces work. It took me
months. I'm not a fool.

GEOFFREY

(Down on one knee next to JOHN.)

I know. Now here's my plan.

JOHN

I read three languages. I've studied law— What plan?

GEOFFREY

We've got to make a deal with Philip.

JOHN

Why?

GEOFFREY

Because you're out and Richard's in.

JOHN

What kind of deal?

GEOFFREY

A war. If we three join and fight now, we can finish Richard off.

JOHN

You mean destroy him?

(GEOFFREY nods.)

And Mother, too?

GEOFFREY

And Mother, too. Well, do we do it? Is it on?

JOHN

I've got to think.

GEOFFREY

You haven't time. We're extra princes now. You know where extra princes go?

JOHN

(Close up as his peril dawns on him.)

Down?

(We go from JOHN's stricken face to—
(PHILIP seated, as before, at the chess table.)

PHILIP

Well? Does John want a war or doesn't he?

(We pull back as GEOFFREY steps forward, protecting JOHN.)

GEOFFREY

Do you? If John asks for your soldiers, will he get them?

PHILIP

If John wants a war, he's got one.

GEOFFREY

John, you hear that?

JOHN

I'm still thinking.

GEOFFREY

Let me help. It's either Richard on the throne or you.

JOHN

(To PHILIP.)

You think we'd win?

PHILIP

I know it.

> (JOHN looks at GEOFFREY, then back to PHILIP, takes a deep breath and resolutely extends his hand. As GEOFFREY and PHILIP formally reach out for a three-way handshake—
>
> (HENRY rises from his place in the Great Hall. The pantomime and laughter still go on as he strides briskly off.
>
> (Down a corridor he goes. ALAIS is with him now, half-running to keep up, as she jabbers at him, pestering.
>
> (She is still at it as the door to the Parlor opens and HENRY strides in.)

ALAIS

But, Henry—

HENRY

I'd appreciate a little quiet confidence. I have enough nits picking at me.

ALAIS

But you've promised me to Richard.

HENRY

Good God, you don't think I meant it?

ALAIS

(Not a bit relieved. If anything, even angrier.)
So that whole scene, all you said to John—

HENRY

You think I'd ever give him up? When I've mothered him
and fathered him and babied him? He's all I've got. How
often do you people have to hear it? Every supper? Should
we start the soup with who we love and who we don't?

ALAIS

I think you like it, passing me from hand to hand. What
am I to you—a collection plate? Or am I all you've got, like
John?

HENRY

(He gets up, starts wandering about the room.
The Christmas decorating and tree trimming has
been completed. Assorted packages are arranged
under the tree. A merry fire burns in the fireplace.
It couldn't be more Christmas Eve.)
I've got to get the Aquitaine for John.

ALAIS

I talk people and you answer back in provinces.

HENRY

They get mixed up. What's the Aquitaine to Eleanor? It's
not a province, it's a way to torture me. That's why she's
spent the evening wooing Richard, wheezing on the coals.
She'll squeeze it out of him. God, I'd have loved to eaves-
drop.

(Doing a creditable imitation of ELEANOR.)
I taught you prancing, lamb, and lute and flute—

(ELEANOR stands in the doorway, a great pile of
Christmas presents in her arms. She can barely see

over the top. She laughs delightedly as she weaves
into the room.)

ELEANOR

That's marvelous. It's absolutely me.

(HENRY goes to her, takes some of the packages.)
I thought as long as I was coming down I'd bring them.

(They move to the Christmas tree.)

HENRY

Whatever are you giving me?

ELEANOR

You're such a child. You always ask.

HENRY

(Reading from a package.)
"To Henry."

(He picks it up, weighs it.)
Heavy.

(Delighted.)
It's my headstone. Eleanor, you spoil me.

ELEANOR

I never could deny you anything.

(She sits at the base of the tree, starts arranging
the boxes just so. Across the room, ALAIS starts to
leave.)

HENRY

Don't go. It nettles her to see how much I need you.

ALAIS

You need me, Henry, like a tailor needs a tinker's dam.

(The deep affection he feels for her is clear on
HENRY's face.)
I know that look. He's going to say he loves me.

HENRY

Like my life.

(She is leaving as HENRY joins ELEANOR on the
floor by the tree.)

I talk like that to keep her spirits up. Well, how'd you do with Richard? Did you break his heart?

ELEANOR

You think he ought to give me back the Aquitaine?

HENRY

I can't think why he shouldn't. After all, I've promised him the throne.

ELEANOR

The boy keeps wondering if your promises are any good.

HENRY

There's no sense asking if the air's good when there's nothing else to breathe.

ELEANOR

Exactly what I told him.

HENRY

Have you got it? Will he give it back?

> (All lightness and movement stop. The cards are down. They remain locked for a moment. Then—)

ELEANOR

No Aquitaine for John.

HENRY

I've got to give him something. Isn't some agreement possible?

> (She breaks the pose, rises to her feet. On top of the situation, enjoying herself.)

ELEANOR

Love, in a world where carpenters get resurrected, anything is possible.

> (HENRY, angry, trying to suppress it, rises, dusts himself off. There is, as in all rooms, straw on the floor.)

HENRY

You bore him, dammit· he's your son.

ELEANOR

Oh, heavens yes. Two hundred eighty days I bore him. I recall them all. You'd only just found Rosamund.

HENRY

Why her so damn particularly? I've found other women.

ELEANOR

Countless others.

HENRY

What's your count? Let's have a tally of the bedspreads you've spread out on.

ELEANOR

Thomas Becket's.

HENRY

(Another raw nerve. Furious.)

That's a lie!

ELEANOR

I know it.

(Amused and musing.)

You still care what I do.

HENRY

(In an outburst of rage.)

I want the Aquitaine for John! I want it and I'll have it!

ELEANOR

Is that menace you're conveying? Is it to be torture? Will you boil me or stretch me, which? Or am I to be perforated?

(HENRY storms to the desk, grabs a pile of papers.)

HENRY

I have the documents and you will sign.

ELEANOR

How can you force me to? Threats? Sign or I refuse to feed you? Tears? Oh, sign before my heart goes crack. Bribes, offers, deals?

> (They are on opposite sides of the desk, leaning
> across it toward each other.)

I'm like the earth, old man; there isn't any way around
me.

HENRY

I adore you.

ELEANOR

Save your aching arches. That road's closed.

> (They exchange looks. HENRY breaks it by sitting
> at his desk, leaning back, very much at ease.)

HENRY

I've got an offer for you, *ma jolie*.

ELEANOR

A deal, a deal. I give the richest province on the Continent
to John for what? You tell me, mastermind. For what?

> (HENRY, close up. Relishing it.)

HENRY

> (Dropping his bomb with quiet precision.)

Your freedom.

> (ELEANOR close up. She has just received a ter-
> rible blow.)

ELEANOR

Oh.

> (HENRY moves around the desk to her as he
> says:)

HENRY

Once Johnny has the Aquitaine, you're free. I'll let you out.
Think: on the loose in London, winters in Provence, im-
promptu trips to visit Richard anywhere he's killing people.
All that for a signature.

ELEANOR

You're good.

> (She backs away as he nears her, stopping with

her back to a charming crèche lit by flickering
candles.)

HENRY

I thought it might appeal to you. You always fancied
traveling.

ELEANOR

Yes, I did. I even made poor Louis take me on Crusade.
How's that for blasphemy? I dressed my maids as Amazons
and rode bare-breasted halfway to Damascus. Louis had a
seizure and I damn near died of windburn but the troops
were dazzled. Henry, I'm against the wall.

(There is no pleasure on HENRY's face.)

To be a prisoner, to be bricked in when you've known the
world—I'll never know how I've survived. These ten years,
Henry, have been unimaginable. And now you offer me the
only thing I want if I give up the only thing I treasure.

(HENRY, sensing victory, picks the papers up.)

HENRY

Sign them and we'll break the happy news. The Queen is
free, John gets the Aquitaine and Richard marries Alais.

(We look from face to face. Will she give in or
won't she?)

ELEANOR

Yes. Let's have it done. I'll sign.

(Delight floods HENRY's face. He bends over the
desk, fiddling with the papers as ELEANOR moves
to the desk chair and sits.)

On one condition.

HENRY

Name it.

ELEANOR

Have the wedding now.

(HENRY is absolutely flummoxed.)

HENRY

What's that?

ELEANOR

Why, I've surprised you. Surely it's not sudden. They've been marching down the aisle for sixteen years and that's a long walk. John can be the best man—that's a laugh— and you can give the bride away. I want to watch you do it.

HENRY

Alais—I can live without her.

ELEANOR

And I thought you loved her.

HENRY

So I do.

ELEANOR

Thank God. You frightened me: I was afraid this wouldn't hurt.

HENRY

You fill me full of fear and pity: what a tragedy you are.

ELEANOR

I wonder, do you ever wonder if I slept with Geoffrey?

HENRY

With my father?

ELEANOR

It's not true but one hears rumors. Don't you ever wonder?
        (The tension spirals. One of them is going to
        explode.)

HENRY

Is it rich, despising me? Is it rewarding?

ELEANOR

No—it's terrible.

HENRY

Then stop it!

ELEANOR

How? It's what I live for!

HENRY

> (Exploding, hurling it at her.)

Rosamund, I loved you!

> (ELEANOR's reaction is triumph. He is ready to strike her. Instead, he storms toward the door, roaring:)

I'll show you! By Christ, I will! I'll do it!

> (He throws open the door, bellows into the hallway:)

Where's a priest? Somebody dig me up a priest!

> (SERVANTS are standing formally in the hallway. WILLIAM MARSHAL is among them. He hurries forward to HENRY.)

You. Bring me a bishop.

> (ELEANOR appears in the doorway behind HENRY. She addresses MARSHAL.)

ELEANOR

Get old Durham. He's just down the hall.

> (As MARSHAL bows, turns to go.)

Ask him to meet us in the chapel.

HENRY

> (Roaring:)

John! Richard! Geoffrey!

> (He storms off down the hall. ELEANOR follows serenely after. SERVANTS scatter, running off to find the boys.
> (We see SERVANTS running. Then brief shots of JOHN, PHILIP, GEOFFREY, RICHARD and ALAIS as each turns sharply, startled. Then—
> (The BISHOP OF DURHAM in his bed. A SERVANT, trying to be both reverential and quick about it, is shaking him awake. The BISHOP is full of food and

wine and years; he knows something important is up and, as he tries focusing on what it is, we—

(Glimpse JOHN, RICHARD, GEOFFREY, PHILIP and ALAIS as they race along, tearing upstairs, downstairs, through halls and corridors.

(In the central hallway, HENRY is pacing, fidgeting and fuming. ELEANOR, calm and composed, stands watching him. HENRY turns abruptly as one by one, RICHARD, JOHN, GEOFFREY, PHILIP and ALAIS come hurrying into the hall through various doors. JOHN reaches HENRY first. As he pulls up in front of his father, breathless, skidding to a stop:)

JOHN

What's wrong? What's happened?

ELEANOR

Richard's getting married.

(The camera moves across all faces as they absorb the startling news.)

JOHN

Now? He's getting married now?

ELEANOR

I never cease to marvel at the quickness of your mind.

JOHN

You can't hurt me, you bag of bile, no matter what you say.

(Moving to HENRY, supplicating.)

But you can. Father, why?

HENRY

Because I say so.

(MARSHAL slips in through the large door.)

MARSHAL

My lord, the bishop's waiting in the chapel.

(HENRY dismisses him with a brusque gesture.)

HENRY

Good. Let's get this over with.

> (He strides forward, throws open a door that
> gives onto a corridor. He storms off. ELEANOR moves
> to ALAIS as they all hurry after him.)

ELEANOR

You'll make a lovely bride. I wonder if I'll cry.

ALAIS

You sound as if you think it's going to happen.

ELEANOR

And I do.

ALAIS

He's only plotting. Can't you tell when Henry's plotting?

ELEANOR

Not this time.

ALAIS

He'll never give me up.

HENRY

You think I won't?

ALAIS

Because you told me so.

HENRY

You're not my Helen. I won't fight a war to save a face.
We're done.

ALAIS

I don't believe you.

HENRY

Wait ten minutes.

> (They go rushing through the Great Hall. It is
> quiet. ALAIS' words are jumbled by panic.)

ALAIS

You don't want me, Richard. Honestly, you don't. We're
not right for each other. Our marriage wouldn't work.
We're not in love, we'd never be happy. . . .

(All at once, we're at the Chapel. HENRY drags
ALAIS up the stairs, throws open the doors. He pulls
her in. The others hurry after. Once inside, they
form a straight line, shoulder to shoulder, across
the back of the Chapel. Through this, ALAIS carries
on.)

Not yet. Oh, please not yet.

(As HENRY all but drags her back toward
her place.)

I won't do it. I won't say the words, not one of them.

(The procession stands at the foot of the aisle,
behind the last pew. The chapel is an exquisite, intimate place. Candles burn, shedding soft, warm
light. The BISHOP OF DURHAM stands waiting on
the altar. HENRY, settling ALAIS into position, casts
an embarrassed-father look toward DURHAM.

(DURHAM smiles back with paternal understanding.

(ALAIS, making one last stab, says:)

Henry, please. It makes no sense. Why give me up? What
do you get? What are you gaining?

HENRY

(With vast innocence as, rather like a bridal con-
sultant, he checks over the bridal party.)

Why, the Aquitaine, of course.

(We take in their faces. JOHN's puzzlement,
GEOFFREY's amusement, ELEANOR's dismay, RICHARD's
dawning rage. RICHARD moves to HENRY.)

RICHARD

What's that again?

HENRY

Your mother gets her freedom and I get the Aquitaine.

(To ELEANOR.)

That is the proposition, isn't it? You did agree.

RICHARD

Of course she did. I knew, I knew it. It was all pretense.
And I believed you. I believed it all.

ELEANOR

I meant it all.

RICHARD

No wedding. There will be no wedding.

> (HENRY throws DURHAM a look of excruciating
> parental embarrassment as he draws RICHARD aside
> and whispers.)

HENRY

But, my boy. Look—Durham's waiting.

> (DURHAM is beginning to look a bit puzzled
> by it all.
> (RICHARD's face is set and stony.)

You've simply got to marry her. It isn't much to ask. For
my sake, Richard.

RICHARD

Never.

HENRY

> (So embarrassed and upset.)

But I've promised Philip. Think of my position.

RICHARD

Damn the wedding and to hell with your position.

HENRY

You don't dare defy me.

RICHARD

Don't I?

> (HENRY throws a glance of badly rattled despera-
> tion in DURHAM's direction, then beckons PHILIP
> forward.)

HENRY

You're the King of France, for goodness sake. Speak up. Do
something.

(RICHARD strides forward as PHILIP approaches.)

RICHARD

Make a threat, why don't you? Scare me.

PHILIP

Dunce.

RICHARD

Am I?

PHILIP

He never meant to have the wedding.

HENRY

Come again?

PHILIP

You're good at rage. I like the way you play it.

HENRY

Boy, don't ever call a king a liar to his face.

PHILIP

I'm not a boy—to you or anybody.

HENRY

Boy, you came here asking for a wedding or the Vexin back. By God, you don't get either one. It's no to both.

PHILIP

You have a pact with France.

HENRY

Then damn the document and damn the French. She never marries, not while I'm alive.

PHILIP

Your life and never are two different times.

HENRY

Not on my clock, boy.

(PHILIP, stiff with anger, turns and strides out of the chapel. ALAIS, weak with relief, leans against the door frame. HENRY is just turning to her when—)

RICHARD

Listen to the lion. Flash a yellow tooth and frighten me.

HENRY

Don't spoil it, Richard. Take it like a good sport.

RICHARD

How's your bad leg and your back and all the rest of it?
You're getting old. One day you'll have me once too often.

HENRY

When? I'm fifty now. My God, boy, I'm the oldest man I
know. I've got a decade on the Pope. What's it to be? The
broadsword when I'm eighty-five?

RICHARD

I'm not a second son. Not now. Your Henry's in the vault,
you know.

HENRY

I know. I've seen him there.

RICHARD

I'll have the crown.

HENRY

You'll have what daddy gives you.

RICHARD

I am next in line.

HENRY

To nothing.

RICHARD

Then we'll have the broadswords now.

HENRY

This minute?

RICHARD

On the battlefield.

HENRY

So we're at war.

RICHARD

Yes, we're at war. I have two thousand men at Poitiers.

HENRY

Can they hear you? Call and see who comes. You are as close to Poitiers as you're going to get.

RICHARD

You don't dare hold me prisoner.

HENRY

Until we've all agreed that John comes next, I can and will.
(RICHARD starts to stalk away.)
You are a king's son so I treat you with respect. You have the freedom of the castle.

RICHARD

(With great bravura as he goes.)
The castle doesn't stand that holds me. Post your guards.
(ELEANOR, ALAIS, HENRY, GEOFFREY and JOHN stand watching him go. Cut to—
(JOHN, close up, as the miracle dawns.)

JOHN

My God, I'm king again. Fantastic. It's a miracle.
(He turns to GEOFFREY.)
Are you happy for me, Geoff?

GEOFFREY

I'm happy for us both.
(GEOFFREY throws a loving arm around JOHN's shoulders as they start out past ELEANOR. We stay with ELEANOR.)

ELEANOR

I came close, didn't I?
(She turns to ALAIS, who stands near her.)
I almost had my freedom and I almost had you for my son. I should have liked it, being free.
(She turns to HENRY. Cut to him. Seated comfortably in a pew, he gives an apologetic shrug and sigh to DURHAM.
(Cut to DURHAM who, both bewildered and

pleased to be dismissed, starts to leave the altar.
        (Cut back to ELEANOR.)
You played it nicely. You were good.

HENRY

        (HENRY stretches out, luxuriating, loving it.)
I really was. I fooled you, didn't I. God, but I do love being
king.

ELEANOR

Well, Henry, liege and lord, what happens now?
        (Cut to HENRY as he rises, moves toward her.)

HENRY

I've no idea. I know I'm winning and I know I'll win,
but what the next move is . . . You're not scared?

ELEANOR

No.

HENRY

I think you are.

ALAIS

        (Moving into the picture.)
I was. You mustn't play with feelings, Henry. Not with
mine.

HENRY

        (Cupping her face in his hands.)
It wasn't possible to lose you. I must hold you dearer than
I thought.
        (He looks up, toward ELEANOR.)
You've got your enigmatic face on. What's your mood, I
wonder.

ELEANOR

Pure delight. I'm locked up with my sons: what mother
doesn't dream of that?
        (She starts toward the door, then stops and
    turns.)
One thing.

HENRY

Yes?

ELEANOR

May I watch you kiss her?

> (We see the three of them. ELEANOR is in the
> background, framed in the doorway.)

HENRY

Can't you ever stop?

ELEANOR

I watch you every night. I conjure it before I sleep.

HENRY

Leave it at that.

ELEANOR

My curiosity is intellectual. I want to see how accurate I am.

> (HENRY opens his arms to ALAIS.)

HENRY

Forget the dragon in the doorway: come.

> (ALAIS moves into his arms.)

Believe I love you, for I do. Believe I'm yours forever, for
I am. Believe in my contentment and the joy you give me
and believe—

> (HENRY, close up as he breaks, turns toward
> ELEANOR.)

You want more?

> (ELEANOR's eyes burn at him. He stares back,
> then turns to ALAIS.)

I'm an old man in an empty place. Be with me.

> (She raises her lips to his. They kiss tenderly at
> first, then passionately. The camera moves across
> their faces, ELEANOR always in the background. The
> sound of caroling grows louder as we begin moving
> closer to ELEANOR's face. She watches and she
> watches.

> (We move past her, out into the courtyard. Lit-

tle fires burn in the midnight darkness. Everything
is still. Here and there, a huddled figure edges
closer to the flames. Though there is quiet now,
there is no peace. Slowly, we move across the yard.
High in a tower, pale light flickers out from one
small window.

(ELEANOR. She is seated at a table in her room,
alone. She has been putting on jewelry for quite
some time. Rings, bracelets, necklaces; she is covered with the stuff. Her face looks ravaged. As
she puts the necklace on, she says:)

ELEANOR

How beautiful you make me. What might Solomon have
sung had he seen this.

(There is a mirror on the table. She starts to
pick it up, then stops.)

I can't. I'd turn to salt.

(Mask slipping for a moment.)

I've lost again. I'm done for now.

(Finding the mask again.)

Well, there'll be other Christmasses.

(She takes an extremely elaborate necklace from
the chest. Addressing it.)

I'd hang you from the nipples but you'd shock the children.

(She puts it on. For a moment, her pain shows
clearly.)

They kissed sweetly, didn't they?

(Hardening again as she leans over the jewel
chest.)

I'll have him next time. I can wait. Ah—there you are:

(Cut to the crown in the chest. Voice over.)

my comfort and my company.

(Her hands appear. She picks the crown up.)

We're locked in for another year: four seasons more. Oh, what a desolation, what a life's work.

> (GEOFFREY appears in the doorway some distance behind her. She turns, smiling brightly as she puts the crown on. She already wears a small coronet and the effect of two crowns on at once is a little mad.)

Is it too much? Be sure to squint as you approach. You may be blinded by my beauty.

GEOFFREY

Merry Christmas.

ELEANOR

Is that why you're here—to tell me that?

GEOFFREY

I thought you might be lonely.

> (ELEANOR removes the crown, holds it out to him.)

ELEANOR

Here, Chancellor. Try it on for size.

GEOFFREY

It's puzzling. I remember my third birthday. Not just pictures of the garden or the gifts, but who did what to whom and how it felt. My memory stretches back that far and never once can I remember anything from you or Father warmer than indifference. Why is that?

ELEANOR

I don't know.

GEOFFREY

That was not an easy question for me and I don't deserve an easy answer.

ELEANOR

There are times I think we loved none of our children.

GEOFFREY

Still too easy, don't you think?

(He is by the table, looking down at her. They are close.)

ELEANOR

I'm weary and you want a simple answer and I haven't one.
(She reaches up, gently touches his cheek.)
I am so sick of all of you.
(JOHN pops jauntily into the room.)

JOHN

I thought I'd come and gloat a little.
(ELEANOR starts removing jewelry.)

ELEANOR

Mother's tired. Come stick pins tomorrow morning. I'll be more responsive then.

JOHN

It's no fun goading anyone tonight.
(RICHARD storms into the room.)

RICHARD

The bastard's boxed us up.
(ELEANOR, utterly unconcerned, goes on removing jewels.)

ELEANOR

What's that, dear?
(RICHARD strides over to her.)

RICHARD

We're his prisoners, if that interests you.

ELEANOR

Why should it? I'm his prisoner anyway.

RICHARD

It was—correct me if I'm wrong—but it was my impression that you wanted Henry's throne for me.

ELEANOR

We've lost it this time, Richard. We can't win.

RICHARD

You think I'm finished, do you?

ELEANOR

So I do. I've suffered more defeats than you have teeth. I know one when it happens to me. Take your wormwood like a good boy. Swallow it and go to bed.

RICHARD

I will be king.

ELEANOR

And so you will. But not this year. Oh, leave it, Richard. Let it go for now.

RICHARD

I can't.

(JOHN *is across the room.*)

JOHN

It's not so hard. Try saying after me: "John wins, I lose."

(RICHARD *starts across the room to* JOHN.)

RICHARD

What if John died?

(JOHN *registers instant panic.*)

JOHN

You wouldn't dare.

RICHARD

Why on earth wouldn't I?

(RICHARD'S *hand moves to his dagger.* JOHN *races across the room to the protection of his mother.*)

JOHN

A knife. He's got a knife.

ELEANOR

Of course, he has a knife. He always has a knife. We all have knives. It is eleven eighty-three and we're barbarians.

(*Her eyes rake across her children.*)

How clear we make it. Oh, my piglets, we're the origins of war. Not history's forces nor the times nor justice nor

the lack of it nor causes nor religions nor ideas nor kinds
of government nor any other thing.

We are the killers; we breed war.

We carry it, like syphilis, inside.

Dead bodies rot in field and stream because the living ones
are rotten.

> (We see them all as she draws them close to-
> gether.)

For the love of God, can't we love one another just a little?
That's how peace begins. We have so much to love each
other for. We have such possibilities, my children. We could
change the world.

> (They want to be loved. She wants to love them.
> As she starts to reach out for RICHARD, GEOFFREY
> says:)

GEOFFREY

And while we hugged each other, what would Philip do?

JOHN

> (In total dismay.)

Oh, good God, Philip. We're supposed to start a war. If
Father finds out, I'll be ruined.

> (JOHN starts for the door. GEOFFREY joins him.)

GEOFFREY

Steady, John; don't panic.

JOHN

Some adviser you are.

> (JOHN hurries from the room as GEOFFREY says:)

GEOFFREY

Don't do anything without me. Let me handle it.

ELEANOR

> (She is alive again.)

He's made a pact with Philip.

> (To GEOFFREY as he joins them.)

You advised John into making war. That peerless boy! He's

disinherited himself. When Henry finds out, when I tell him what John's done—I need a little time. Can you keep John away from Philip 'til I say so?

GEOFFREY

Anything you say.

> (He kisses her hand and bounds from the room as she turns to RICHARD.)

ELEANOR

I want you out of here before this breaks. And that needs Philip. Go to him. Be desperate, promise anything: the Vexin, Brittany. Then once you're free and John is out of favor, we'll make further plans.

RICHARD

You talk to Philip. You're the diplomat; you see him.

ELEANOR

You're a friend. You know him; I don't.

> (RICHARD looks at her expressionlessly, then starts to the door.)

And Richard.

> (He stops in the doorway.)

Promise anything.

> (We see RICHARD close up. He either loves his mum or loathes her. This is loathing. As he turns and goes—
>
> (We move to ELEANOR alone in the center of the room. As she turns round full circle:)

I haven't lost. It isn't over. Oh, I've got the old man this time. The damn fool thinks he loves John. He believes it. That's where the knife goes in.

> (Close up, all triumph gone.)

Knives, knives . . . it was fine thought, wasn't it? Oh, Henry, we have done a big thing badly.

> (She starts to look for something. We follow her gaze about the room.

Where's that mirror? I am Eleanor and I can look at anything.

> (The camera finds the mirror. Her hand appears, picks the mirror up. We see her reflection, wavy and distorted in the primitive glass.)

My, what a lovely girl.

> (The camera moves from the reflection to her face.)

How could her king have left her?

> (We hold on her face. Then, suddenly, we see—
> (A door. A hand appears, taps lightly on it and we hear:)

GEOFFREY

> (Whispering.)

Philip?

> (PHILIP, preparing for bed, stands in shirtsleeves in his bedroom. The room is more luxuriously furnished than the others in the castle, PHILIP having brought his own refinements with him. There is a canopy bed. Wine glasses and decanter sit on a table.
> (PHILIP turns sharply as we see him. He moves to the door, opens it. GEOFFREY slips in, closes it behind him. He is keyed high; quiet, tense, excited.)

It's working out. By morning I can be the chosen son. The crown can come to me. Are you still with me?

> (PHILIP nods.)

We'll have to fight them all. They'll band together once this happens. Have I got your word?

PHILIP

Do I have yours? All England's land in France if I support you?

> (GEOFFREY nods. PHILIP looks at him speculatively.)

GEOFFREY

Are we allies, then?

PHILIP

> (Warmly taking his hand.)

We were born to be.

GEOFFREY

I should say something solemn but I haven't time.
> (Halfway to the door.)

I'm off to Father with the news that John's a traitor. After
that—

> (JOHN, livid, charges out from behind a tapestry.)

JOHN

You stink, you know that? You're a stinker and you stink.
> (GEOFFREY doesn't bat an eye.)

GEOFFREY

Come along. We're finished here.
> (Looking wildly about the room.)

JOHN

I'll kill you. Where's a dagger?

> (He can't find anything. Then, seeing a lethal-
> looking, massive candlestick, he grabs it, raises it
> it high over his head and charges at GEOFFREY.

> (GEOFFREY crouches slightly as JOHN comes tear-
> ing at him. At the last moment, GEOFFREY sidesteps
> gracefully, tripping JOHN as he hurtles by.

> (JOHN sprawls out painfully on the floor. GEOF-
> FREY glares at him, anger and derision on his face.)

GEOFFREY

Dumb. If you're a prince, there's hope for every ape in Africa.
> (He goes to one knee beside JOHN as JOHN sits
> up.)

I had you saved. I wasn't on my way to Father but he was.
He would have gone to Henry and betrayed you. Look: it's
in his face.

>(JOHN looks up.)

JOHN

>(Convinced and dismayed.)

It's true. I don't know who my friends are.

>(There is a tapping at the door. PHILIP and GEOF-
>FREY exchange a quick glance.

>(RICHARD is in the corridor. He darts a look
>one way, then the other. Satisfied he's still alone, he
>raps again and whispers:)

RICHARD

Philip.

>(GEOFFREY bounds to his feet and indicating the
>tapestry where JOHN was hidden, asks:)

GEOFFREY

May we?

PHILIP

That's what tapestries are for.

>(PHILIP starts toward the door. GEOFFREY tugs
>JOHN to his feet, bustles him toward the tapestry.)

JOHN

I've ruined everything. I'll never learn.

>(JOHN and GEOFFREY duck behind the tapestry.
>(We see PHILIP standing by the door.)

PHILIP

Is someone there? I heard my name.

>(He opens the door. RICHARD stands in the door-
>way.)

RICHARD

I called it.

PHILIP

Richard. Hello, Richard.

RICHARD

You're halfway to bed. I'll wait for morning.

PHILIP

Come in.

> (He moves into the room. We stay with RICHARD
> in the doorway.)

RICHARD

Mother sent me.

PHILIP

Come in anyway.

> (He picks up the decanter, pours. RICHARD moves
> into the picture.)

Our alchemists have stumbled on the art of boiling bur-
gundy. It turns to steam and when it cools, we call it
"brandywine."

RICHARD

I'm Henry's prisoner.

> (PHILIP smiles.)

You find that charming?

PHILIP

No.

RICHARD

Then why the charming smile?

PHILIP

I thought, I can't think why, of when you were in Paris last.
Can it be two whole years ago?

RICHARD

It can. I need an army, Philip.

> (PHILIP hands him a glass.)

PHILIP

It will take the cold away.

RICHARD

I must have soldiers.

> (PHILIP strolls away, moving casually about the
> room.)

PHILIP

Have I aged? Do I seem older to you? They've been two
fierce years. I've studied and I've trained to be a king.

RICHARD

I'll have your answer—yes or no.

> (PHILIP spins sharply toward RICHARD.)

PHILIP

You'll have it when I give it.

> (Charming again, he moves across the room to
> RICHARD.)

You see? I've changed. I'm not the boy you taught to hunt
two years ago. Remember? Racing after boar, you flying first,
me scrambling after, all day into dusk—

> (RICHARD turns abruptly away from him, starts
> to go.)

Don't go.

RICHARD

I must know: Will you help me?

> (PHILIP sits in one of the chairs by the table.)

PHILIP

Sit and we'll discuss it.

> (RICHARD moves to the other chair and sits stiffly.)

You never write.

RICHARD

To anyone.

PHILIP

Why should I make you King of England? Aren't I better
off with John or Geoffrey? Why have you to fight when I
could have the cretin or the fiend?

(Behind the tapestry, JOHN is indignant, GEOF-
FREY amused.)

RICHARD

Would we fight?

PHILIP

We're fighting now. Good night.

(He starts to rise, the interview terminated.)

RICHARD

You're still a boy.

PHILIP

In some ways. Which way did you have in mind?

RICHARD

You haven't asked how much your help is worth.

PHILIP

You'll tell me.

RICHARD

You can have the Vexin back.

PHILIP

And what else?

RICHARD

All of Brittany.

(Behind the tapestry, GEOFFREY is angry now
and JOHN amused.)

PHILIP

That's Geoffrey's.

RICHARD

Does that matter?

PHILIP

Possibly to Geoffrey. And what else?

RICHARD

That's all your help is worth.

PHILIP

And in return, what do you want from me?

RICHARD

Two thousand soldiers.

PHILIP

And what else?

RICHARD

Five hundred knights on horse.

PHILIP

And what else?

RICHARD

Arms and siege equipment.

PHILIP

And what else?

RICHARD

I never wrote because I thought you'd never answer.

(PHILIP is expressionless.)

You got married.

PHILIP

Does that make a difference?

RICHARD

Doesn't it?

PHILIP

I've spent two years on every street in hell.

RICHARD

That's odd. I didn't see you there.

(PHILIP rises, eyes on RICHARD. Then RICHARD stands. Slowly, PHILIP extends his hand. RICHARD takes it. PHILIP turns and, in measured step, starts moving toward the bed. RICHARD, still holding his hand, follows.

(The interior of the bed. PHILIP's hand comes through the curtains, draws them back. We see them through the opening.)

You haven't said you loved me.

PHILIP

When the time comes.

> (There is a tapping at the door. PHILIP and
> RICHARD paralyzed, exchange startled glances.
>
> (HENRY is in the corridor. He glances about.
> Then raps again and whispers:)

HENRY

Philip.

> (At the bed, RICHARD is in great confusion.
> PHILIP is thinking hard.
>
> (Behind the tapestry, JOHN, frightened, turns to
> GEOFFREY. GEOFFREY, alive with excitement, puts a
> finger on JOHN's lips.
>
> (PHILIP puts a finger to RICHARD's lips, helps him
> into the bed. PHILIP draws the curtains shut, moves
> to the door and opens it.)

HENRY

Philip, lad.
It's not too late at night?

PHILIP

I'd hoped you'd come.

HENRY

> (We see the room from HENRY's point of view as
> he enters.)

Good; we can't leave negotiations where they are.

> (Turning to PHILIP, who moves to the table and
> pours from the decanter.)

I keep looking for your father in you.

PHILIP

He's not there.

> (We see them both as HENRY settles in RICHARD's
> chair.)

HENRY

I miss him. Has Richard or the Queen been here to see you?

PHILIP

Does it matter? If they haven't yet, they will.

HENRY

I want to reach a settlement. I left you with too little earlier.

> (PHILIP hands HENRY a glass, sits in the other
> chair.)

PHILIP

Yes; nothing is too little.

HENRY

I'm sorry you're not fonder of me, lad. Your father always said, "Be fond of stronger men."

PHILIP

No wonder he loved everyone.

HENRY

I've come to you to offer peace.

PHILIP

Piss on your peace.

HENRY

Your father would have wept.

PHILIP

My father was a weeper.

HENRY

Fight me and you'll lose.

PHILIP

I can't lose, Henry. I have time. Just look at you. Great heavy arms. Each year they get a little heavier. The sand goes pit-pat in the glass. I'm in no hurry, Henry. I've got time.

> (HENRY rises, angry.)

HENRY

Suppose I hurry things along? What if I say that England is at war with France?

> (PHILIP calmly looks up at HENRY.)

PHILIP

Then France surrenders. I don't have to fight to win. Take all you want—this county, that one. You won't keep it long.

HENRY

(Scornful)

What kind of courage have you got?

PHILIP

(Cool and unperturbed.)

The tidal kind: it comes and goes.

(HENRY breaks out into a delighted smile and sits again. We see them both.)

HENRY

By God, I'd love to turn you loose on Eleanor.

(The decanter in his hand.)

More brandywine?

PHILIP

You recognize it?

HENRY

(Filling his glass.)

They were boiling it in Ireland before the snakes left.

(Sitting back, settling in his chair.)

Well—things look a little bleak for Henry, don't they? You'll say yes to Richard when he comes; arms, soldiers, anything he asks for.

PHILIP

I'd be foolish not to.

HENRY

And withdraw it all before the battle ever started.

PHILIP

Wouldn't you, in my place?

HENRY

Why fight Henry when his sons will do it for you?

PHILIP

Yes, exactly.

HENRY

You've got promise, lad. That's first-class thinking.

PHILIP

Thank you, sir.

> (HENRY raises his glass and drinks.
>
> (RICHARD, in the bed, looks angry and betrayed.
>
> (We see behind the tapestry, more anger and betrayal.
>
> (HENRY wipes his lips and puts his glass down.)

HENRY

Good night.

> (HENRY rises. PHILIP looks up, uncertain for the first time.)

PHILIP

Good night? You're going?

> (HENRY nods benignly.)

But we haven't settled anything.

HENRY

We open Christmas packages at noon. 'Til then.

> (HENRY starts to go. PHILIP rises.)

PHILIP

You can't be finished with me.

HENRY

But I am. And it's been very satisfactory.

PHILIP

What's so satisfactory?

HENRY

Winning is. I did just win. Surely you noticed.

PHILIP

Not a thing. You haven't won a damn thing.

> (We see them both as HENRY moves slowly to PHILIP, saying:)

HENRY

I found out the way your mind works and the kind of man

you are. I know your plans and expectations. You have
burbled every bit of strategy you've got. I know exactly what
you will do and exactly what you won't. And I've told you
exactly nothing. To these aged eyes, boy, that's what winning looks like. *Dormez bien.*

> (With which he turns and, as we follow him,
> moves toward the door.)

PHILIP

You—

> (HENRY stops and turns.)

You made my father nothing. You were always better. You
bullied him, you bellied with his wife, you beat him down
in every war, you twisted every treaty, you played mock-
the-monk and then you made him love you for it.

> (He begins stalking toward HENRY.)

I was there. His last words went to you.

HENRY

He was a loving man and you learned nothing of it.

PHILIP

I learned how much fathers live in sons. A king like you
has policy prepared on everything. What's the official line
on sodomy? How stands the crown on boys who do with
boys?

> (We see RICHARD in the bed, disbelief, shock on
> his face. It can't be happening.
>
> (HENRY moves away from PHILIP.)

HENRY

Richard finds his way into so many legends. Let's hear yours
and see how it compares.

> (As PHILIP speaks, he follows HENRY, pressing
> him.)

PHILIP

He found me first when I was fifteen. We were hunting. It
was nearly dark. My horse fell. I was thrown. I woke to

Richard touching me. He asked me if I loved him—"Philip, do you love me?"—and I told him yes.

> (RICHARD in the bed. He is wracked with pain and rage. It is excruciating.
>
> (PHILIP bears down harder.)

You know why I told him yes? So one day I could tell you all about it. You cannot imagine what that "yes" cost. Or perhaps you can. Imagine snuggling to a chancred whore and, bending back your lips in something like a smile, saying: "Yes, I love you and I find you beautiful." I don't know how I did it.

> (RICHARD leaps through the curtains.)

RICHARD

No—it wasn't like that!

PHILIP

(Cold and cutting.)

But it was.

RICHARD

You loved me.

PHILIP

Never.

> (RICHARD turns to HENRY.)

RICHARD

Get out. Please! I don't want you here.

HENRY

It's no great joy to be here.

RICHARD

So the royal corkscrew finds me twisted, does he?

HENRY

I'll go tell your mother: she'll be pleased.

> (He starts to go. RICHARD follows him.)

RICHARD

She knows. She sent me.

HENRY

(Turning on RICHARD. They stand face to face.)
How completely hers you are.

RICHARD

You've had four sons. Who do you claim? Not Henry. Not
my buried brother. Not that monument to muck, that epic
idiot. Why him? Why always him and never me?

HENRY

He was the oldest—he came first.

RICHARD

Christ, Henry, is that all?

HENRY

You went with Eleanor.

RICHARD

You never called for me. You never said my name. I would
have walked or crawled. I'd have done anything.

(HENRY turns away, unable to face it.)

HENRY

It's not my fault. I won't be blamed.

RICHARD

I only wanted you.

HENRY

No—it's my crown. You want my kingdom.

RICHARD

Keep your kingdom.

(HENRY wheels toward RICHARD.)

HENRY

That I will!

RICHARD

I hope it kills you!

HENRY

Thank God I have another son. Thank God for John.

(GEOFFREY steps out from behind the tapestry.)

GEOFFREY

Who shall we thank for Geoffrey?
(Moving to HENRY.)
You don't think much of me.

HENRY

Much? I don't think of you at all.

GEOFFREY

Nurse used to say I had your hands. I might have had more
of you. Try seeing me. I haven't Richard's military skill but
he was here betraying you, not I. I haven't John's I don't
know what—God knows what you can see in John—and he's
betrayed you, too.
(JOHN, red with rage, peeps through a slit in the
tapestry.)

HENRY

You think I'd ever make you king?

GEOFFREY

You'll make me king because I'm all you've got.
(Pointing at RICHARD.)
I was to be his chancellor. Ask him why.

HENRY

(Starting to leave the room.)
I've heard enough.

GEOFFREY

For moving John to treason.

HENRY

I don't doubt he offered, I don't doubt you tried and I don't
doubt John loves me.
(GEOFFREY steps to the tapestry.)

GEOFFREY

Like a glutton loves his lunch.
(He pulls the tapestry back, revealing JOHN.
JOHN glares at GEOFFREY with pure loathing.)

JOHN

You turd.

HENRY

Well, John?

JOHN

It isn't what you think.

HENRY

What do I think?

JOHN

What Geoffrey said. I wouldn't plot against you, ever.

HENRY

I know; you're a good boy.

> (JOHN, encouraged, moves toward HENRY. Just
> JOHN and HENRY now.)

JOHN

Can I go now, please? It's late. I ought to be in bed.

> (HENRY grabs JOHN by the shoulders, shakes
> him.)

HENRY

Couldn't you wait? Couldn't you trust me? It was all yours.
Couldn't you believe that?

JOHN

Will you listen to the grief?

HENRY

Who do you think I built this kingdom for?

> (JOHN, in a rage, shakes himself loose.)

JOHN

Me? Daddy did it all for me? When can I have it, Daddy?
Not until we bury you?

HENRY

You're just like them. And after all I've given you.

JOHN

I got it. I know what you gave.

HENRY

I loved you.

JOHN

You're a cold and bloody bastard, you are, and you don't love anything.

> (HENRY is stunned, blank with shock.)

GEOFFREY

I'm it, I'm all that's left.
Here, Father; here I am.

> (We move toward HENRY, closer and closer to his
> unseeing eyes.)

HENRY

My life, when it is written, will read better than it lived. Henry Fitz-Empress, first Plantagenet, a king at twenty-one, the ablest soldier of an able time. He led men well, he cared for justice when he could and ruled, for thirty years, a state as great as Charlemagne's. He married out of love a woman out of legend. Not in Rome or Alexandria or Camelot has there been such a queen. She bore him many children—but no sons. King Henry had no sons.

> (Cut to JOHN, RICHARD and GEOFFREY side by side.
> Then back to HENRY.)

He had three whiskered things but he disowned them. You're not mine. We're not connected. I deny you. None of you will get my crown. I leave you nothing and I wish you plague. May all your children breech and die.

> (He turns, moves to the doorway, stops and looks
> back.)

My boys are gone.

> (HENRY starts unsteadily down the corridor.)

I've lost my boys.

> (He stops, glares up toward the Deity.)

You dare to damn me, do You? Well, I damn You back.

(Like a Biblical figure, shaking his fist at the sky.)

God damn You.

(Moving blindly down the corridor again.)

My boys are gone. I've lost my boys. Oh, Jesus, all my boys.

(We follow him as, stunned and stumbling, he moves painfully through his quiet, darkened castle. He pauses in the Parlor doorway, not seeing the Christmas tree and presents and the embers in the fireplace. We see him in the doorway of his bedroom, uncertain where he is.

(ALAIS, still in bed, starts at the sight of him. Alarmed, she starts to rise. He turns and leaves. She follows to the bedroom door, looks after him, love and concern for her man mingled on her face.

(We see him all alone, high on the ramparts of his castle. The night is clear and bitter cold. He looks down at the river bank. ELEANOR's barge, empty and dark, is there.

(We see him lying down on icy stones. He doesn't feel the cold. He looks up unblinking at the sky. The picture fades.)

(We come up slowly on a tiny bed of gently glowing coals, very close up. As we see them, we hear:)

ALAIS

(Singing.)

The Christmas wine is in the pot,
The Christmas coals are red.
I'll spend my day the lover's way,
Unwrapping all my gifts in bed.

(As she sings, we pull slowly back. The coals are in a small copper brazier. On the brazier, we see a small pot. ALAIS's hands appear. One holds a

tiny spice jar; the other takes a pinch of spice and
drops it in the pot.

(We continue back as we see ALAIS sitting on the
floor by the brazier. Then we see HENRY's bedroom beyond her and, at the last, ELEANOR standing
in the doorway. She looks absolutely desolate.)

The Christmas Mass is over now,
The Christmas—

(She stops singing as she senses someone. She
turns.

(We see her pull herself together. As if nothing
in the world were wrong, she moves into the room
saying:)

ELEANOR

No one else is caroling tonight: it might as well be Lent.
When I was little, Christmas was a time of great confusion
for me. The Holy Land had two kings, God and Uncle
Raymond, and I never knew whose birthday we were cele-
brating.

(Reaching ALAIS, she looks fondly down at her.)

ALAIS

Henry isn't here.

ELEANOR

Good; we can talk behind his back.

ALAIS

What happened?

ELEANOR

Don't you know?

(ALAIS shakes her head. ELEANOR sits on the floor
by her.)

There was a scene with beds and tapestries and many things
got said.

(She leans forward over the pot on the brazier.)

Spiced wine. I'd forgotten Henry liked it. May I stay?

ALAIS

(She rises, puts the spice pot on a table.)

It's your room just as much as mine: we're both in residence.

ELEANOR

Packed in, like the poor, three to a bed.

ALAIS

Did you love Henry—ever?

ELEANOR

Ever? Back before the flood?

ALAIS

As long ago as Rosamund.

ELEANOR

Ah, that's prehistory, lamb; there are no written records or survivors.

ALAIS

There are pictures. She was prettier than you.

ELEANOR

Oh, much. Her eyes in certain light were violet and all her teeth were even. That's a rare fair feature, even teeth. She smiled to excess but she chewed with real distinction.

ALAIS

And you hate her even now.

ELEANOR

No . . . but I did. He put her in my place, you see, and that was very hard. Like you, she headed Henry's table: that's my chair.

ALAIS

And so you had her poisoned.

ELEANOR

No, I never poisoned Rosamund. Oh, I prayed for her to drop and sang a little when she did. . . . Why aren't you happy? Henry's keeping you. You must be cleverer than I am.

ALAIS

I've tried feeling pity for you but it keeps on turning into something else.

ELEANOR

Why pity?

ALAIS

You love Henry but you love his kingdom, too. You look at him and you see cities, acreage, coastline, taxes. All I see is Henry. Leave him to me, can't you?

ELEANOR

But I left him years ago.

ALAIS

And I thought I could move you. Were you always like this? Years ago, when I was young and worshiped you, is this what you were like?

ELEANOR

Most likely. Child, I'm finished and I've come to give him. anything he asks for.

ALAIS

Do you know what I should like for Christmas? I should like to see you suffer.

ELEANOR

(The suffering clear on her face.)

Alais, just for you.

> (ALAIS understands and all the love and tenderness she used to feel for ELEANOR come flooding back. With a small cry, she throws herself into ELEANOR's arms. ELEANOR holds her, rocks her, like a child, gently back and forth.)

ALAIS

Maman, ô Maman.

ELEANOR

Alors, ma petite.

ALAIS

J'ai peur, Maman.

> (Still rocking, ELEANOR starts to hum ALAIS' little
> song. Then something catches her eye. She stops
> humming, turns.
>
> (HENRY stands in the doorway. He sees them but
> he doesn't really take them in. His manner is brisk,
> keyed high, with a kind of mad energy.)

HENRY

The sky is pocked with stars. What eyes the wise men must
have had to spot a new one in so many.

> (ALAIS rises and moves to the wine pot on the
> brazier.)

ELEANOR

You look cold.

ALAIS

I've mulled some wine.

> (HENRY moves into the room.)

HENRY

I wonder, were there fewer stars then? I don't know. I fancy
there's a mystery in it.

> (ALAIS moves into the picture with a goblet of
> wine.)

What's this?

ALAIS

Warm wine.

HENRY

Why, so it is.

> (He takes the wine, touches her cheek.)

You are as beautiful as I remembered.

> (Sending her toward the door.)

Off to bed. My widow wants to see me.

> (ALAIS moves closer to him.)

ALAIS

Let me stay.

HENRY

I won't be long.

ALAIS

She came to find out what your plans are.

HENRY

I know that.

ALAIS

She wants you back.

HENRY

Go to your room.

>   (ALAIS turns slowly and goes. HENRY moves to his
>   chair by the fireplace and sits.)

So you want me back.

ELEANOR

>   (Settling in a chair on the other side of the fire-
>   place.)

She thinks I do. She thinks the need for loving never stops.

HENRY

She's got a point. I marvel at you. After all these years, still like a democratic drawbridge, going down for everybody.

ELEANOR

At my age, there's not much traffic any more.

>   (He raises his goblet in a toast.)

HENRY

To your interminable health.

>   (He drinks.)

Well, wife, what's on your mind?

ELEANOR

Oh Henry, we have made a mess of it.

HENRY

Yes, haven't we? You look like doomsday.

ELEANOR

Late nights do that to me. Am I puffy?

HENRY

Possibly: it's hard to tell.

ELEANOR

I've just seen Richard.

> (We see them both, flanking the fireplace. The
> logs burn low and warm.)

HENRY

Splendid boy.

ELEANOR

He says you fought.

HENRY

We always do.

ELEANOR

It's his impression that you plan to disinherit them.

HENRY

I fancy I'll relent. Don't you?

ELEANOR

I don't much care.

> (HENRY turns sharply to face her.)

In fact I wonder, Henry, if I care for anything. I wonder if
I'm hungry out of habit and if all my lusts, like passions
in a poem, aren't really recollections.

HENRY

I could listen to you lie for hours. So your lust is rusty. Gorgeous.

ELEANOR

Henry, I'm so tired.

> (HENRY rises, starts moving toward her.)

HENRY

Sleep, then. Sleep and dream of me with *croûtons. Henri à
la mode.*

(As he reaches her, she rises with a surge of energy.)

ELEANOR

Henry, stop it.

HENRY

Eleanor, I haven't started.

ELEANOR

What is it you want? You want my name on paper, I'll sign anything. You want the Aquitaine for John? It's John's. It's his, it's yours, it's anybody's.

HENRY

In exchange for what?

ELEANOR

For nothing, for a little quiet, for an end to this, for God's sake, sail me back to England, lock me up and lose the key and let me be alone.

(HENRY nods appreciatively. Then, raising his hands, he starts to applaud.

(The applause grows louder and louder.)

You have my oath. I give my word.

(The applause grows thunderous, then cuts off abruptly. Bone weary, nodding, ELEANOR sinks into a chair.)

Oh, well. Well, well.

(HENRY circles her like a dog that's trapped its prey.)

HENRY

Would you like a pillow? Footstool? How about a shawl? Your oaths are all profanities. Your word's a curse. Your name on paper is a waste of pulp.

(She is not reacting. He bends toward her, bellowing:)

I'm vilifying you, for God's sake! Pay attention!

(She looks up, only half seeing.)

ELEANOR

How, from where we started, did we ever reach this Christmas?

HENRY

Step by step.

ELEANOR

What happens to me now?

(We follow HENRY as he moves away from her.)

HENRY

That's lively curiosity from such a dead cat. If you want to know my plans, just ask me.

ELEANOR

Conquer China, sack the Vatican or take the veil. I'm not among the ones who give a damn. Just let me sign my lands to John and go to bed.

(HENRY stretches out luxuriously in his chair.)

HENRY

No, you're too kind. I can't accept.

(ELEANOR moves to the chair, glares down at him.)

ELEANOR

Come on, man. I'll sign the thing in blood or spit or bright blue ink. Let's have it done.

HENRY

Let's not. No, I don't think I want your signature on anything.

ELEANOR

You don't?

HENRY

Dear God, the pleasure I still get from goading you.

ELEANOR

You don't want John to have my provinces?

HENRY

Bull's eye.

(She bends down over him.)

ELEANOR

I can't bear you when you're smug.

(HENRY grins up at her, reveling in it.)

HENRY

I know, I know.

(She straightens up, draws slightly back.)

ELEANOR

You don't want Richard and you don't want John.

HENRY

You've grasped it.

ELEANOR

All right, let me have it. Level me. What do you want?

HENRY

(Savoring each syllable.)

A new wife.

(ELEANOR, close up. She is utterly dismayed.)

ELEANOR

Oh.

(She sits slowly on the floor by his chair.)

So I'm to be annulled. Well, will the Pope annul me, do
you think?

HENRY

The Pontif owes me one Pontificate. I think he will.

ELEANOR

Out Eleanor, in Alais. Why?

HENRY

A new wife, wife, will bear me sons.

(ELEANOR rises, glaring down at him.)

ELEANOR

That is the single thing of which I should have thought you
had enough.

(He rises. They stand face to face.)

HENRY

I want a son.

ELEANOR

Whatever for? Why, we could populate a country town
with country girls who've borne you sons. How many is it?
Help me count the bastards.

HENRY

All my sons are bastards.

ELEANOR

You really mean to do it.

HENRY

Lady love, with all my heart.

>   (HENRY turns away from her, moves energetically
>   to a narrow slit of a window, stands with his back
>   to her, looking out.)

ELEANOR

Your sons are part of you.

HENRY

Like warts and goiters; and I'm having them removed.

ELEANOR

We made them. They're our boys.

HENRY

I know—and good God, look at them. Young Henry: vain,
deceitful, weak and cowardly. The only patriotic thing he
ever did was die.

ELEANOR

I thought you loved him most.

HENRY

I did.

>   (He turns to face her.)

And Geoffrey—there's a masterpiece. He isn't flesh: he's a
device; he's wheels and gears.

ELEANOR

Every family has one.

HENRY

But not four. Then Johnny. Was his latest treason your idea?
(She shakes her head.)
I have caught him lying and I've said he's young. I've seen
him cheating and I've thought he's just a boy. I've watched
him steal and whore and whip his servants and he's not a
child. He is the man we've made him.

ELEANOR

Don't share John with me. He's your accomplishment.

HENRY

And Richard's yours. How could you send him off to deal
with Philip?

ELEANOR

I was tired. I was busy. They were friends.

HENRY

Eleanor, he was the best. And from the cradle on you cradled
him. I never had a chance.

ELEANOR

You never wanted one.

HENRY

How do you know? You took him. Separation from your
husband you could bear. But not your boy.

ELEANOR

Whatever I have done, you made me do.

HENRY

You threw me out of bed for Richard.

ELEANOR

Not until you threw me out for Rosamund.

HENRY

It's not that simple. I won't have it be that simple.

ELEANOR

I adored you.

HENRY

Never.

ELEANOR

I still do.

(Cut to HENRY, close up.)

HENRY

Of all the lies, that one is the most terrible.

(Cut to ELEANOR, close up.)

ELEANOR

I know: that's why I saved it up for now.

(Their eyes lock, blazing. Neither moves. Then,
suddenly, they throw themselves into each other's
arms. They hold tight, wanting shelter from the
storm they've made.)

Oh, Henry, we have mangled everything we've touched.

HENRY

Deny us what you will, we have done that.

(He pulls away from her, looks gently down into
her face.)

Do you remember when we met?

ELEANOR

(Looking radiantly up at him.)

Down to the hour and the color of your stockings.

HENRY

I could hardly see you for the sunlight.

(She settles on the floor. He goes down close
beside her.)

ELEANOR

It was raining but no matter.

HENRY

There was very little talk as I recall it.

ELEANOR

Very little.

HENRY

I had never seen such beauty and I walked right up and

touched it. God, where did I find the gall to do that?

>   (She bends tenderly toward him.)

ELEANOR

In my eyes.

HENRY

I loved you.

>   (They kiss, then gently part, each lost in reverie.)

ELEANOR

No annulment.

HENRY

What?

ELEANOR

There will be no annulment.

HENRY

Will there not?

ELEANOR

No, I'm afraid you'll have to do without.

HENRY

>   (Anger just bottled in.)

Well—it was just a whim.

ELEANOR

I'm so relieved. I didn't want to lose you.

HENRY

Out of curiosity, as intellectual to intellectual, how in the name of bleeding Jesus can you lose me? Do you ever see me? Am I ever with you? Ever near you? Am I ever anywhere but somewhere else?

>   (ELEANOR, close up, delighted. HENRY's rage
>   mounts.)

Do we write? Do I send messages? Do dinghies bearing gifts float up the Thames to you? Are you remembered?

ELEANOR

You are.

HENRY

You're no part of me. We do not touch at any point. How can you lose me?

ELEANOR

Can't you feel the chains?

HENRY

You know enough to know I can't be stopped.

ELEANOR

But I don't have to stop you. I have only to delay you. Every enemy you have has friends in Rome. We'll cost you time.

HENRY

(Rising, backing away from her.)

What is this? I'm not moldering; my paint's not peeling off. I'm good for years.

ELEANOR

(On her feet, pursuing him.)

How many years? Suppose I hold you back for one? I can— it's possible. Suppose your first son dies? Ours did—it's possible. Suppose you're daughtered next? We were—that, too, is possible. How old is daddy then? What kind of spindly, ricket-ridden, milky, semiwitted, wizened, dim-eyed, gammy-handed, limpy line of things will you beget?

HENRY

It's sweet of you to care.

ELEANOR

And when you die, which is regrettable but necessary, what will happen to frail Alais and her pruney prince? You can't think Richard's going to wait for your grotesque to grow.

HENRY

You wouldn't let him do a thing like that?

ELEANOR

Let him? I'd push him through the nursery door.

HENRY

You're not that cruel.

ELEANOR

Don't fret. We'll wait until you're dead to do it.

(HENRY moves to her, into the picture.)

HENRY

Eleanor, what do you want?

ELEANOR

(Beating down on him with great intensity.)

Just what you want: a king for a son. You can make more.
I can't. You think I want to disappear? One son is all I've
got and you can blot him out and call me cruel. For these
ten years you've lived with everything I've lost and loved
another woman through it all. And I'm cruel. I could peel
you like a pear and God himself would call it justice.

HENRY

I will die sometime soon. One day I'll duck too slow and
at Westminster they'll sing out "Long Live the King" for
someone else. I beg you, let it be a son of mine.

ELEANOR

I am not moved to tears.

HENRY

(Desperate.)

I have no sons.

ELEANOR

You have too many sons. You don't need more.

(He glares at her. She glares back. There is a
strong sense of stalemate. Just as we think there
is nothing either can do, HENRY breaks into a broad
and terrible smile.)

HENRY

Well, wish me luck. I'm off.

(He turns, strides toward the door.)

ELEANOR

To Rome?

HENRY

>(Not pausing, moving out of the room into the corridor.)

That's where they keep the Pope.

>(She follows him into the corridor.)

ELEANOR

You don't dare go.

>(HENRY stops and turns to face her.)

HENRY

Say that again at noon, you'll say it to my horse's ass. Lamb, I'll be rid of you by Easter. You can count your reign in days.

ELEANOR

You go to Rome, we'll rise against you.

HENRY

Who will?

ELEANOR

Richard, Geoffrey, John and Eleanor of Aquitaine.

HENRY

The day those stout hearts band together is the day that pigs get wings.

ELEANOR

There'll be pork in the treetops come the morning. Don't you see? You've given them a common cause: new sons. You leave the country and you've lost it.

HENRY

All of you at once.

ELEANOR

And Philip, too. He'd join us.

HENRY

Yes, he would.

ELEANOR

Now how's your trip to Rome?

(HENRY seems cornered, beaten.)

Oh, I've got you, got you, got you.

HENRY

Should I take a thousand men-at-arms or is that showy?

ELEANOR

Bluff away. I love it.

> (He starts moving forward toward her. She begins retreating. We keep with them as they edge their way back into the bedroom.)

HENRY

Ah, poor thing. How can I break the news? You've just miscalculated.

ELEANOR

Have I? How?

HENRY

You should have lied to me. You should have promised to be good while I was gone. I would have let your three boys loose. They could have fought me then.

ELEANOR

You wouldn't keep your sons locked up here?

HENRY

Why the devil wouldn't I?

ELEANOR

> (Desperate.)

You don't dare.

HENRY

> (Unstoppable, victorious.)

Why not? What's to stop me? Let them sit in Chinon for a while.

> (We see them both.)

ELEANOR

I forbid it!

> (Cut to HENRY.)

HENRY

She forbids it!

    (He storms toward the door.)

ELEANOR

Did your father sleep with me or didn't he?

    (HENRY stops. Color drains from his face. It is a
    thought he cannot bear. He turns toward her.)

HENRY

No doubt you're going to tell me that he did.

ELEANOR

Would it upset you?

HENRY

    (Stalking toward ELEANOR.)

What about the thousand men? I say be gaudy and to hell
with it.

ELEANOR

    (Retreating, she finds herself against his bed.)

Don't leave me, Henry. I'm at rock bottom. I'll do anything
to keep you.

HENRY

I think you think you mean it.

    (We see them both, their faces close together. She
    is kneeling on the bed.)

ELEANOR

Ask for something.

HENRY

Eleanor, we're past it; years past.

ELEANOR

Test me. Name an act.

HENRY

There isn't one.

ELEANOR

About my fornication with your father—

HENRY

Yes, there is. You can expire.

ELEANOR

You first, old man. I only hope I'm there to watch. You're so afraid of dying. You're so scared of it.

HENRY

Poor Eleanor; if only she had lied.

ELEANOR

(She sits on the bed, starts to stretch out.)

She did. She said she never loved your father.

HENRY

I can always count on you.

ELEANOR

I never touched you without thinking "Geoffrey, Geoffrey."

(She lies back moving sensuously. He crouches over her.)

HENRY

When you hurt me, I'll cry out.

ELEANOR

I've put more horns on you than Louis ever wore.

HENRY

Am I supposed to care?

ELEANOR

I'll kill you if you leave me.

HENRY

You can try.

(She leans up, close to him.)

ELEANOR

I loved your father's body. He was beautiful.

HENRY

(Retreating from the impact of it, sitting on the edge of the bed, turning away from her.)

It never happened.

ELEANOR

I can see his body now. Shall I describe it?

HENRY

Eleanor, I hope you die.

> (She rises to her knees on the bed, seeming to
> tower over him.)

ELEANOR

His arms were rough, with scars here—

HENRY

Stop it!

ELEANOR

I can feel his arms. I feel them.

HENRY

> (Crying out.)

Aahhh!

ELEANOR

What's that? Have I hurt you?

> (He rises like a stricken animal, stumbles blindly
> against a table, falls, keeps on moving, wriggling,
> crawling toward the door. She is on her feet, loom-
> ing over him in terrible triumph. He drags himself
> somehow to his feet and staggers through the
> door. She rushes toward the doorway.)

ELEANOR

> (Hurling it after him.)

We did it! You were in the next room when he did it!

> (She reaches the door frame, leans against it for
> support, sinks to the floor, her face a picture of
> total desolation.)

Well, what family doesn't have its ups and downs?

> (Eyes moving aimlessly about.)

It's cold.

I can't feel anything. Not anything at all.

We couldn't go back, could we, Henry?

> (We fade slowly on her desolate and anguished
> face. The moment we reach black—

> (A great hand slapping down with tremendous
> impact on the buttocks of a body asleep in bed.
> There is a howl of surprised pain as the body bolts
> upright and we pull back to reveal—

> (HENRY, a flaming torch in hand, looming over
> WILLIAM MARSHAL, who is wide awake, naked to
> the waist in bed. HENRY is bursting with energy,
> his eyes bright.

> (HENRY, torch in hand, strides down a crude stone
> barracks room. Sleeping soldiers in uniforms lie
> on the floor. MARSHAL follows HENRY along.)

HENRY

> (More a bellow than a word.)

Hey—hey—hey.

> (General stirring as SOLDIERS wake up.)

When the King is off his ass, nobody sleeps.

> (A SQUAD OF SOLDIERS, MARSHAL in command,
> strides down a corridor. They halt beside a door.

> (Interior of the room. JOHN and sad-faced
> SERVANT GIRL are in bed, covered up, naked. JOHN
> is asleep, his head on her breast. She is awake,
> pathetic eyes staring sadly at nothing.

> (In the corridor. MARSHAL gestures an order.
> TWO SOLDIERS break ranks, move to the door.
> MARSHAL gestures again and the SQUAD moves down
> the corridor.

> (SERVANT GIRL sees something, gasps in fear as
> rough hands appear in the picture. The hands hurl
> back the blankets. JOHN's eyes fly open. His scream
> of terror is cut off as a hand covers his mouth.

> (GEOFFREY lies in bed, awake. Cool and clear as

always, he is busy thinking. He hears a sound. Only his eyes move. None of the panic that he feels shows in his face.

(A thick door opens. MARSHAL, in the corridor, stands in the doorway. Cautiously, he enters. We follow his gaze as he takes in RICHARD's room. It is empty. Tense, he advances. We see RICHARD crouched behind the door in back of him.

(RICHARD makes his move, lunging for the open door. SOLDIERS block his way. He turns back. MARSHAL's sword is leveled at his throat.

(A dungeon-like place. Vague shapes and shadows. JOHN, GEOFFREY and RICHARD are hurled into view. A great door clanks closed. A candle burns. The boys pick themselves up. We follow them in candle light as, crouching and tense, they start exploring the mysterious and vast cellars of the castle.

(HENRY, with his torch, strides into the vast kitchen of the castle. MARSHAL follows after him. Fires glow in fireplaces. VASSALS lie asleep on the floor amidst carcasses of beef and poultry and the day's debris. HENRY strides among them, kicking them awake.

(We see HENRY, striding through the poultry yard outside, kicking chickens, ducks and geese awake. The CHICKEN KEEPER, half asleep, stands listening to orders from MARSHAL. There is much honking and squawking.

(We see HENRY, close up, bending over coals at the SMITH's forge. His energy seems manic; sweat pours off his face. He is looking at a glowing piece of metal, part of a suit of armor. The ARMORER brings his hammer crashing down.

(HENRY and MARSHAL stride across the courtyard.

All about him, shadowy figures are stirring. MEN
are pushing a heavy wagon. Horses neigh. Still
with his torch, he pauses, looks up at a tower. A
light comes from ELEANOR's window.)

HENRY

Tell her to pack. She's leaving when it's light out.

(MARSHAL nods and strides off. As HENRY plunges
back into the melee of the yard, we see—

(ELEANOR in her bedroom, dressed for travel. Before her, on the table, is the jewel chest. Behind her,
in the background, her two MAIDS-IN-WAITING are
busy packing clothes.

(ELEANOR is tense with concentration. There must
be some move that she can make, some gambit . . .
Her fingers drum nervously on the table.)

(Back in the yard, we get the sense that HENRY
is everywhere. We see him pushing, heaving, lift-
ing, swearing. SOLDIERS march past, SERVANTS race
about us, horses whinny as they strain at wagons,
dogs howl.

(ELEANOR's room again. Still at her table, fingers
drumming, she looks up. Her GUARD appears. She
looks at him more closely. Then, eyes bright, she
comes to a decision.

(Outside, HENRY pauses in the melee of the yard.
Close up, he looks a little mad. His eyes are red,
his face smudged. He seems to vibrate with ner-
vous energy. He tears a great chunk from a loaf
of bread and, devouring it, makes for his castle.

(Lunging down a corridor he goes. He grabs a
door, hurls it thunderously open and strides into a
room. ALAIS, dressed as we saw her last, lies curled
up, sound asleep. She jumps as the door bangs,
wide awake.)

ALAIS

Henry? What's wrong?

HENRY

We're packing up and moving out.

ALAIS

Is there a war? What's happened?
          (He throws his arms around her in a great bear
     hug.)
Henry, what's the matter?

HENRY

Nothing, for a change. Would you believe it?

ALAIS

Where've you been all night?

HENRY

Out making us an entourage.

ALAIS

What for?

HENRY

We're off to Rome to see the Pope.

ALAIS

He's excommunicated you again.

HENRY

He's going to set me free. I'm having Eleanor annulled. The
nation will be shocked to learn our marriage wasn't con-
summated.

ALAIS

Oh, be serious.

HENRY

I am. It seems that you and I are getting married.
By the Pope himself.

ALAIS

You mean it?

HENRY

Shall I kneel?

ALAIS

It's not another trick?

HENRY

The bridal party's drilling on the cobblestones.

ALAIS

She still loves you, Henry.

HENRY

So she says.

ALAIS

She'll find a way to stop us.

HENRY

How? She won't be here. We're launching her for Salisbury Tower when the winds change. She'll be barging down the River Vienne by lunchtime.

ALAIS

If she doesn't stop us, Richard will.

HENRY

Not any more. I've corked him up. He's in the cellar with his brothers and the wine. The royal boys are aging with the royal port. You haven't said yes. Would you like a formal declaration?

> (He goes to one knee, turning his profile to us.)

There—my finest angle; it's on all the coins. Sad Alais, will you marry me?

> (She looks down at him lovingly.)

Be my Queen.

> (She goes down to him, melts in his arms. He kisses her cheeks, her hands, her neck.)

We'll love each other and you'll give me sons. Let's have five—we'll do Eleanor one better. Why, I'll even call the first one Louis, if you like. Louis le Premier: how's that for a King of England?

> (They start to laugh. They try to kiss but both of them are laughing. Gradually, as HENRY roars

on, her laughter subsides, then stops, all joy fading
from her face.)

ALAIS

Henry—you can't ever let them out.

HENRY

(Laughter subsiding.)

You've lost me. Let who out?

ALAIS

Your sons. You've put them in the dungeon and you've got
to keep them there forever.

HENRY

Do I now?

ALAIS

If they're free when you die, it's the dungeon or the nunnery
for me. I don't care which—a cell's a cell—but, Henry, what
about the child.

HENRY

(Anger beginning, he gets to his feet.)

Don't bother me about the child. The damn thing isn't born
yet.

(Furious, he wheels about and starts to go.)

ALAIS

Henry?

(Near the door, he stops. She moves to him.)

Are you going down?

(He nods.)

To let them out or keep them in?

HENRY

Could you say to a child of yours, "You've seen the sun
light for the last time"?

ALAIS

Can you do it, Henry?

HENRY

I shall have to, shan't I?

(ALAIS watches him go, both elated and aghast at what she has accomplished. She hesitates, then runs out of the room after him.

(HENRY comes bounding down the broad stone steps to the courtyard. ALAIS appears at the top of the steps, hesitates again, then hurries after him.

(We watch them moving through the yard. The troup of ACTORS wanders blearily into the picture. We lose HENRY and ALAIS as, for a moment, we follow the ACTORS along, leaving them as we pick up ELEANOR in a corner of the yard. She carries the jewel chest. Her GUARD follows along behind.

(ELEANOR goes down a flight of stone steps, moving from daylight into gloom. Her GUARD follows.

(ELEANOR moves down a dark, twisting corridor. She reaches another flight of steps, starts down. Her GUARD follows.

(The wine-cellar door. The SOLDIER stands by it in the recess, alert. We pull back, taking in the curve of the corridor. ELEANOR rounds the curve, stops and draws back.

(She turns to her GUARD. He is very close to her now. She nods. They exchange a look of understanding. The GUARD draws a short, blunt, heavy dagger and starts stealthily forward.

(We see them all: ELEANOR tensely watching; her GUARD edging forward, pressed along the curving wall; the SOLDIER in the recess, unaware but listening.

(ELEANOR'S GUARD stops just before the recess. He crouches, ready to leap. Both he and the SOLDIER wear armor from the waist up. The GUARD raises his dagger. His armor squeaks.

(The SOLDIER spins at the sound. The GUARD

leaps. His knife flashes down, glancing harmlessly on the SOLDIER's armor. They face each other in the confines of the recess. There is no room. They feint, armor making the moves heavy and slow. The SOLDIER lunges. His dagger slides and scrapes along the GUARD's armor, searching for a point of entry. The only sounds are natural ones: grunts, heavy breathing, the clank and rattle of armor, the squeal of dagger points on steel. It's all so clumsy. Every move is graceless. Nothing works. The walls keep getting in the way. They wheeze and stumble. It is ludicrous—and it is this that gives the fight its special horror.

(ELEANOR's GUARD is thrown clear of the recess. He lunges back. They fall, rolling and clanking about in the shadowed niche. Slow-moving arms and thrashing legs. We pull back to include ELEANOR. She wills herself to watch. There is a strangled cry. One pair of legs goes into spasm. She goes on watching as her GUARD rises, keys to the door in hand.

(Deep in the wine cellar, we find JOHN, RICHARD and GEOFFREY. JOHN lies sprawled out, asleep. RICHARD, apparently placid, lies staring at nothing. GEOFFREY sits, tense, his face a picture of concentration. The tiny candle on the floor is guttering out. Echoing down long corridors comes the distant rattle of chains and bolts on the cellar door. JOHN wakes with a start. The others stiffen.

(They exchange looks as the sound of the closing door reverberates and dies. RICHARD is the first to rise.)

                    RICHARD

He's here.

(The others get to their feet. There is nothing to
say. RICHARD starts into a low, dark, twisting corridor. The others follow. It is very dark. The corridor curves and curves. We follow as they twist
along. Softly, really to himself, RICHARD mutters.)

He'll get no satisfaction out of me. He isn't going to see
me beg.

GEOFFREY

Why, you chivalric fool—as if the way one fell down
mattered.

RICHARD

When the fall is all there is, it matters.

(They go around a corner. Far ahead of them,
we make out an area of brighter light.

(RICHARD, the others just behind him, moves into
brighter light. He registers surprise.

(ELEANOR is standing in the center of the large
room near the cellar door. Several candles flicker
on the walls. She carries the jewel chest.)

ELEANOR

My barge is leaving any minute and I've come to say good-
bye.

GEOFFREY

Does Henry know you're here?

ELEANOR

I've brought you each a little something.

GEOFFREY

What's he planning?

RICHARD

Is he going to keep us here?

ELEANOR

(Moving toward a crude wooden table.)

I picked them out especially.

RICHARD

For God's sake, Mother—

> (She slams the chest down on the table. It makes
> a heavy, menacing, metallic clatter.
>
> (RICHARD looks at ELEANOR.
>
> (At once he's at the chest, throwing it open.
> We see a clutter of blunt, heavy, brutal-looking
> daggers.
>
> (RICHARD turns toward ELEANOR.)

RICHARD

How heavy is the outside guard?

ELEANOR

That's taken care of.

RICHARD

What about the courtyard and the gates?

ELEANOR

They're putting Henry's train together and it's chaos. You
can walk right out.

RICHARD

> (Moving to JOHN and GEOFFREY.)

We'll go to Poitiers. He'll expect that but we'll meet him
with an army when he comes. Keep close to me and, when
you run, run hard.

GEOFFREY

Why run at all? I think we ought to stay.

JOHN

Stay here?

GEOFFREY

'Til Henry comes.

> (He turns toward ELEANOR. Cut to her. Voice
> over.)

He will come, won't he—

> (Turning back to his brothers.)

—and he'll come alone. I count three knives to one.

RICHARD

You think we could?

JOHN

I'd only do it wrong. You kill him and I'll watch.

GEOFFREY

The three of us together. We must all three do it.
(ELEANOR moves angrily to them.)

ELEANOR

You don't think I'm going to let this happen?

GEOFFREY

If you tell, there'll be a rash of executions and you don't
want that. No, you don't want to lose a one of us: not even
me.

ELEANOR

You're clever but I wonder if you're right.

GEOFFREY

You warn him, it's the end of us: you warn him not and
it's the end of him. It's that clear.

ELEANOR

(She turns to Richard.)
Take the knives and run.

RICHARD

No. Geoffrey's right; we'll stay.

ELEANOR

You, too? Oh, Richard.

RICHARD

(Striding to the knives.)
Spare me that. You brought these things.
(He picks one up, holds it out toward her.)
You want him dead, you do it.
(Cut to ELEANOR, close up. Spitting it at him.)

ELEANOR

You unnatural animal.
(RICHARD starts moving slowly toward ELEANOR.

When he gets close to her, she starts edging away, back toward the dank stone walls. He follows, pressing her.)

RICHARD

Unnatural, Mummy? You tell me, what's Nature's way? If poisoned mushrooms grow and babies come with crooked backs, if goiters thrive and dogs go mad and wives kill husbands, what's unnatural? Here stands your lamb. Come cover him with kisses. He's all yours.

ELEANOR

No, you're not mine. I'm not responsible.

RICHARD

Where do you think I learned this from? Who do you think I studied under? How old was I when you fought with Henry first?

ELEANOR

Young . . . I don't know.

RICHARD

How many battles did I watch?

ELEANOR

But those were battles, not a knife behind a door.

RICHARD

I never heard a corpse ask how it got so cold. What were you thinking when you fought with him?

(She is against the wall now, pressed to the damp stones. He keeps moving in until their faces are inches apart.)

ELEANOR

Of you.

RICHARD

Of your unnatural animal?

ELEANOR

I did it all for you.

RICHARD

You wanted Father dead.

ELEANOR

No, never that.

RICHARD

You tried to kill him, didn't you?

ELEANOR

Yes!

RICHARD

Why?! What did you want?!

ELEANOR

I wanted Henry back.

> (It is an answer he cannot bear. He turns away,
> moving out of the picture.)

RICHARD

You lie.

ELEANOR

I wanted Henry.

> (She looks about, eyes on her children.
> (The sound of chains and bolts being drawn is
> heard. ELEANOR stiffens, tense.
> (The boys freeze.
> (We're at the door as ELEANOR'S GUARD opens it.
> We see HENRY's head only—his face ashen, his eyes
> unblinking, fixed straight ahead—as he passes
> through the door. ALAIS, holding a lighted taper,
> follows.
> (The boys hear the door close. GEOFFREY, the
> first to recover, looks at RICHARD, RICHARD looks
> back, ready to do the deed if GEOFFREY is. Then,
> suddenly, JOHN is running, racing to the chest.
> He slams the lid down just as—
> (HENRY moves into view. He carries a load of

large candles in his arms. ALAIS, holding a lighted
taper, follows him. He pauses, peers about and
then announces:)

HENRY

It wants light.

(He begins moving about the area, placing candles in empty candlesticks. ALAIS follows, lighting
them with her taper. He doesn't seem to see his sons
as he passes by them. They, however, are on wires,
at the brink, not quite sure how or when to make
their move.)

What we do in dungeons needs the shades of day. I stole
the candles from the chapel. No one minded. Jesus won't be-
grudge them and the Chaplain works for me.

(He stops by ELEANOR.)

ELEANOR

You look dreadful.

HENRY

So do you.

ELEANOR

I underslept a little.

HENRY

(We pull back, including them all, as HENRY de-
posits his last candle and steps back to survey the
effect.)

We can all rest in a little while. That's better. Bright and
clear, just like the morning.

(His eyes traveling from son to son, meaning it.)

Fine-looking boys.

RICHARD

(Striding angrily into the picture.)

What do you want from us? You must be mad. Why did
you have to come here? Damn you, why'd you come?

HENRY

You were the best
            (Indicating ELEANOR.)
I told her so.
            (To JOHN.)
You—you, I loved.

RICHARD

You're going to lock us up.
            (HENRY neither nods nor shakes his head.)
You've got to. You can't ever let me out. You know you
can't. I'll never stop.

HENRY

I can't stop either.
            (RICHARD and HENRY stand, eyes locked. RICHARD
            turns sharply away, looks toward—
            (GEOFFREY, close up. He is white with tension.
            Will he do it? Won't he?
            (As for JOHN, he's terrified.
            (RICHARD flies across the room toward the chest.
            (HENRY draws his dagger.
            (RICHARD throws the chest open and grabs a dag-
            ger. He looks at—
            (GEOFFREY. He hasn't moved. Nor is he going to.
            (JOHN is ready to cry.
            (HENRY strides toward RICHARD and chest.)
Brave boys. That's what I've got.
            (At the chest, he picks up a dagger and tosses
            it to GEOFFREY. And another which he tosses to
            JOHN.
            (The boys are spread out in a semicircle. They
            have daggers in hand but none of them moves.
            (HENRY crouches, ready for them all, wanting
            them all to come at him.)

Come on. What is it? Come for me!

> (ALAIS, stiff with fear, stands pressed against a
> wall. ELEANOR, her face a mask, only her eyes alive,
> registers no change as—

> (HENRY starts slowly moving across the room
> toward RICHARD. He stops near him, crouching, his
> dagger held low, close, lethal. RICHARD makes no
> move.)

What's wrong? You're Richard, aren't you?

RICHARD

But you're Henry.

JOHN

> (Near tears.)

Daddy? Take me back? Please? Can't we try again?

HENRY

> (Trying to take in the idea.)

Again?

JOHN

We always have before.

HENRY

Oh, yes . . . we always have.

> (With a cry of joy, JOHN drops his dagger and
> starts running across the room to his father, arms
> outstretched. He skids to a stop and crumples to
> the floor as HENRY, with a terrible animal sound,
> starts for him with his dagger.

> (HENRY, his face dreadful, goes to one knee,
> crouching over his son, ready to shove the dagger
> into JOHN's vitals. The man is absolutely going to
> do the deed.)

ELEANOR

> (Sharp and commanding.)

Go on.

(HENRY turns to look at her as she moves into the picture.)

Execute them. They're assassins, aren't they? This was treason, wasn't it? You gave them life—you take it.

(They exchange a long look. Then HENRY's eyes leave her and travel to his sons.

(They are hardly breathing, save for JOHN, who is whimpering on the floor.

(HENRY's eyes return to ELEANOR.)

HENRY

Who's to say it's monstrous? I'm the king. I call it just.

(HENRY turns from her and, alone now, draws his great sword and strikes a ritualistic, formal pose. His face shines with sweat and his eyes are mad.)

Therefore, I, Henry, by the grace of God, King of the English, Lord of Scotland, Ireland and Wales,

(We see the whole room. JOHN makes little animal sounds of fear. GEOFFREY believes he's done for but is still trying to think of a way out. RICHARD is ready to die with dignity and style.)

Count of Anjou, Brittany, Poitou and Normandy, Maine, Gascony and Aquitaine, do sentence you to death.

(Then to HENRY close up, still in his pose.)

Done this Christmas Day at Chinon in God's year eleven eighty-three.

(As he lowers his sword, we cut back to see them all. In a formal, measured way, HENRY moves across the damp stone floor to RICHARD. It seems a long walk.

(Cut to HENRY and RICHARD, close, as HENRY comes to a stop before him. RICHARD, eyes unswervingly on his father, stands motionless. HENRY

slowly raises his sword—higher, higher—With a
howling cry, HENRY brings the sword whistling
down, flat edge against RICHARD's shoulder. It makes
a stinging slap-crack of a sound.

(RICHARD staggers slightly, masking the pain as
best he can, staring steadily at his father. HENRY's
face is bewildered, as if he has lost contact for a
moment, not knowing where he is or what he's
doing. The moment hangs suspended as the camera
moves to the other faces. JOHN still whimpers, unable to grasp what has happened. GEOFFREY, eyes
bright with anticipation, is still waiting for the
violence. ELEANOR's face tells us nothing at all.
ALAIS' fear changes suddenly to concern as, with a
little gasp, she steps forward, then stops herself.
She is looking at—

(HENRY as, spent and shattered, he sinks slowly
to the floor. He sits there seeing nothing.)

Surely that's not what I intended. Children . . . children are
. . . they're all we have.

(Unable to look at his sons, he waves them from
the room.)

Go on. I'm done, I'm done, I'm finished with you. You and
I are finished. Never come again.

(We draw back to take in the sons. GEOFFREY is
the first to understand. He gives a short, sharp
nod and starts into the shadows toward the cellar
door. JOHN scurries after him. RICHARD hesitates—
as if he had something to say but can't—then follows them out the door.)

ELEANOR

You spare the rod, you'll spoil those boys.

HENRY

(Huddled on the floor.)

I couldn't do it, Eleanor.

ELEANOR

Nobody thought you could.

ALAIS

(Moving tenderly to HENRY.)

Come rest.

HENRY

I want no women in my life.

ALAIS

You're tired.

HENRY

I could have conquered Europe, all of it, but I had women in my life.

(To ALAIS gruffly.)

Get out. Go on. Go.

(ALAIS moves toward the door, out of the picture as HENRY, like a great cat, moves to ELEANOR.)

I should have killed you years ago.

ELEANOR

There's no one peeking. Do it now.

HENRY

You put me here. You made me do mad things. You've bled me.

ELEANOR

Shoulder it yourself. Don't put it on my back. You've done what you have done and no one but yourself has made you do it. Pick it up and carry it. I can. My losses are my work.

HENRY

What losses? I've been cheated, not you. I'm the one with nothing.

ELEANOR

Lost your life's work, have you? Provinces are nothing. Land is dirt.

I've lost you and I can't ever have you back again.

You haven't suffered. I could take defeats like yours and laugh. I've done it. If you're broken, it's because you're brittle. You are all that I have ever loved. Christ, you don't know what nothing is.

> (A shudder passes through her, like a stab of physical pain.)

I want to die.

> (HENRY's initial doubt is followed by terrible dismay.)

HENRY

You don't.

> (She is doubled up by the intensity of it, scarcely able to stand.)

ELEANOR

I want to die.

HENRY

I'll hold you.

> (She shakes her head, edges away.)

It might help.

ELEANOR

> (Lacking the strength to stand, sinking to the floor.)

I want to die.

HENRY

> (Going to one knee beside her.)

Let me do something, damn you. This is terrible.

ELEANOR

Henry, I want to die.

HENRY

You will, you know. Wait long enough and it'll happen.

ELEANOR

(Surprised by a smile she didn't expect.)

So it will.

(He takes her hand.)

HENRY

We're in the cellar and you're going back to prison and my life is wasted and we've lost each other and you're smiling.

ELEANOR

It's the way I register despair. There's everything in life but hope.

HENRY

We have each other and, for all I know, that's what hope is.

ELEANOR

We're jungle creatures, Henry, and the dark is all around us. See them?

(Her eyes range the room.)

In the corners, you can see the eyes.

HENRY

And they can see ours.

(HENRY rises to his feet, a picture of enormous strength and majesty.)

I'm a match for anything. Aren't you?

(ELEANOR looks up at him with the most profound affection.)

ELEANOR

I should have been a great fool not to love you.

(HENRY nods in brisk agreement, bends down, helps her up. They start toward the cellar door.

(We see the prow of ELEANOR's barge. Pulling back, we see HENRY and ELEANOR moving energetically through the mud along the river bank. With surprised delight, ELEANOR is saying:)

ELEANOR

You'll let me out for Easter?

HENRY

Come the Resurrection, you can strike me down again.

ELEANOR

(Alive again, ready for anything.)

Perhaps I'll do it next time.

HENRY

And perhaps you won't.

ELEANOR

It must be late and I don't want to miss the tide.

(She sweeps past him, out onto the boat. Lines are cast off, the OARSMEN dip their oars. The boat begins to ease out into the river.

(On the bank, eyes never for a moment leaving her, HENRY leans forward, shouting)

HENRY

You know, I hope we never die.

ELEANOR

I hope so, too.

HENRY

You think there's any chance of it?

(He starts to laugh. She joins him. The music rises and the boat glides toward the center of the sweeping river. We see his laughing face, then hers, eyes never wavering.

(He throws his arms out in a gesture of animal vitality. The boat moves on. But to the end we can see ELEANOR, unmoving, eyes on HENRY, standing on the shore, arms open to the world.)

By the author of THE COLLECTOR . . .
John Fowles

the magus

"Fascinating . . . from the black of death and dark arts
to the warm, clear tones of flesh and love and a sunny
Greek island . . . a beautiful, broadloom magic carpet."

—*Detroit News*

"Always—and frighteningly—believable . . . wit and
wisdom interwoven in a complex drama which climaxes with
a Sade-like sexual fantasy that outdoes the master."

—*Playboy*

"A sumptuous firework exhibition . . . brilliant."

—*The New York Times Book Review*

A DELL BOOK 95c

See the dazzling 20th Century-Fox movie starring
Anthony Quinn, Michael Caine, Candice Bergen and Anna Karina

The triumphant bestseller

The story of
the love that ended an empire

NICHOLAS AND ALEXANDRA

Here, for the first time, is the intimate account
of the last Tsar of Russia, his lovely, tormented
wife, his four enchanting daughters, and his
only son, a victim of hemophilia, the hereditary
flaw that placed him, and ultimately the fate of
the empire, in the hands of a Siberian mystic.

*"A WONDERFULLY RICH TAPESTRY, the
colors fresh and clear, every strand sewn in with
a sure hand. Mr. Massie describes those strange
and terrible years with sympathy and understanding . . . they come vividly before our eyes."*
—NEW YORK TIMES

*"A larger than life drama, so bizarre, so heart-
rending and, above all, so apocalyptic, that no
novelist would have dared invent it."*
—SATURDAY REVIEW SYNDICATE

A DELL BOOK
with 16 pages of rare photographs
$1.25

The sensational bestseller
by the author of
The Devil's Advocate
and
The Shoes of the Fisherman . . .

MORRIS L. WEST

THE TOWER
OF BABEL

The scene: Israel and the Arab nations surrounding her. The main characters: a hard-bitten Israeli general; a dedicated Arab leader; an amoral international financial wizard; a cynical Jewish double agent; a lovely, tormented Israeli sculptress; and a sensual, pleasure-seeking Frenchwoman. The time: the weeks of intrigue, decision, and explosion that embody all the power, passion and moral dilemma of a world on the razor edge of chaos.

"On one level, a compulsive thriller, charged with intrigue and melodrama. On a different level, a novel engaged with the mysteries of human confusions. West is a mighty storyteller."

—BOOK WORLD

If you cannot obtain copies of this title at your local bookseller, just send the price (plus 10c per copy for handling and postage) to Dell Books, Box 2291, Grand Central Post Office, New York, N. Y. 10017. No postage is required on any order of five or more books.

*The great bestseller
by the author of*
The Tower of Babel
and
The Devil's Advocate . . .

Morris L. West

The Shoes
of the Fisherman

A tremendous drama of faith, courage and momentous intrigue that stretches from the shadows of the Kremlin to the power and the glory of the Vatican.

"A novelistic drama of great power and immediate concern. Brilliant"—Time

Now a towering motion picture starring: Anthony Quinn, Oscar Werner, David Janssen, Vittorio de Sica, Leo McKern, John Gielgud, and Sir Laurence Olivier.

A DELL BOOK • 95c

If you cannot obtain copies of this title at your local bookseller, just send the price (plus 10c per copy for handling and postage) to Dell Books, Box 2291, Grand Central Post Office, New York, N.Y. 10017. No postage or handling charge is required on any order of five or more books.

How many of these Dell Bestsellers have you read?

NICHOLAS AND ALEXANDRA by Robert K. Massie   **$1.25**

THE DOCTOR'S QUICK WEIGHT-LOSS DIET
by I. Maxwell Stillman and S. Sinclair Baker   **95c**

ROSEMARY'S BABY by Ira Levin   **95c**

THE DEAL by G. William Marshall   **95c**

SEVENTH AVENUE by Norman Bogner   **95c**

THE PRESIDENT'S PLANE IS MISSING
by Robert J. Serling   **95c**

THE KLANSMAN by William Bradford Huie   **95c**

OUR CROWD by Stephen Birmingham   **$1.25**

THE FIXER by Bernard Malamud   **95c**

GO TO THE WIDOW-MAKER by James Jones   **$1.25**

BASHFUL BILLIONAIRE by Albert B. Gerber   **95c**

THE SHOES OF THE FISHERMAN by Morris L. West   **95c**

THE LAWYERS by Martin Mayer   **$1.25**

MY SILENT WAR by Kim Philby   **95c**

If you cannot obtain copies of these titles at your local bookseller, just send the price (plus 10c per copy for handling and postage) to Dell Books, Box 2291, Grand Central Post Office, New York, N.Y. 10017. No postage or handling charge is required on any order of five or more books.